The Lord Is My Shepherd

For Judy

With Blessings –

Rabbi: A M Lew

The Lord Is My Shepherd

PSALMS TO ACCOMPANY US
ON OUR JOURNEY THROUGH AGING

Albert Micah Lewis

William B. Eerdmans Publishing Company

Grand Rapids, Michigan / Cambridge, U.K.

Wm. B. Eerdmans Publishing Co.

255 Jefferson Ave. S.E., Grand Rapids, Michigan 49503 /
P.O. Box 163, Cambridge CB3 9PU U.K.

Printed in the United States of America

07 06 05 04 03   5 4 3 2 1

Library of Congress Cataloging-in-Publication Data

Lewis, Albert Micah.
The Lord is my shepherd:
Psalms to accompany us on our journey through aging /
Albert Micah Lewis.
p.   cm.
ISBN 0-8028-4982-2 (pbk.)
1. Bible. O.T. Psalms XXIII — Meditations.
2. Bible. O.T. Psalms XCVIIII — Meditations.
3. Bible. O.T. Psalms CXXI — Meditations.
4. Christian aged — Prayer-books and devotions — English.
I. Title.

BS1450 23rd.L49   2003
223′.206 — dc21

2002035405

www.eerdmans.com

To Shirley Kane Lewis,

life partner and
earthly guardian of my soul

CONTENTS

———∞∞∞———

Contents
———
viii

PREFACE

The origins of the book of Psalms are shrouded in mystery. Scholars throughout the Jewish and Christian communities have long studied these pieces of poetry, philosophy, and theology, and they continue to discuss and debate when, where, and by whom they were written. Some scholars have attributed all or some of the psalms to the time of King David (1004-965 BCE [Before the Common Era]); others to a later time during the Babylonian Exile (586-539 BCE); and others to the still later Maccabean Period (167-63 BCE). Indeed, many more books have been written about the psalms than there are psalms! All of this scholarship, meditation, and reflection on the psalms testifies to the fact that the psalms express a deep and abiding meaning in Jewish and Christian life.

We yearn to understand God's words, and the psalms have something to say to us at every age, at every stage of our life's journey.

This book is specifically meant for older people to help them reflect on this particular stage of their journey through life and to allow the psalms to nourish them on their journey. While I will refer to the wisdom that can be gleaned from a number of both Jewish and Christian sources, older as well as contemporary, my primary goal is to explore three psalms — Psalm 121, Psalm 23, and Psalm 98 — to see how they might speak helpfully to those of us who are, in the wonderful biblical phrase, "full of years." I invite you to read these psalms through the lens of your own life experience and to reflect on your past journey, your present life, and the rich possibilities that lie before you in whatever your particular circumstances are now. Perhaps you are living as a couple — or alone — in an apartment or condominium or retirement home. Perhaps you are in a nursing home. As you read, you will gain, I hope, an abundance of rich Jewish and Christian insights. Together we will examine each of these psalms, line by line, discover often overlooked meanings, and seek spiritual reassurance and peace, as have so many generations before us.

Each psalm is presented first in the King James Version. The KJV is the translation most familiar to many older Christian readers and is especially beloved for the great beauty of its language. It is also easily recognizable to the Jewish reader. Following the King James Version is my own translation based on ancient and modern Hebrew interpretations. On the opening title page for each psalm, the first line of the psalm is also presented in the traditional Hebrew characters. For those of you who are unfamiliar with Hebrew, this will introduce you to the look of this ancient language in its original form. And for those of you who are acquainted with Hebrew, this will provide a sense of familiarity and comfort. In the Jewish tradition, it should be noted, the very shape of the Hebrew characters is often thought to carry meaning. In fact, according to a particular Jewish mystical tradition, simply contemplating the Hebrew letters for YHVH — the letters that make up God's name — can, as our eye enters and moves through the characters, lead us into a more intimate relationship with God. If you wish to see the complete Hebrew text for each psalm, you may turn to the end of the book. In addition to the full texts in Hebrew characters, I have also provided there a "transliteration" of each of the psalms, which means a rendering of the Hebrew characters in the letters with which you are familiar. This will allow those who do not know Hebrew to nonetheless hear and recite the sounds. I have used these same transliterations when I have referred in my text to specific Hebrew words. Finally, at the end of the book you will also find a list of books to which I refer in the text, in case you would like to explore some of these texts further.

For every psalm, the discussion of each line (or set of lines) is followed with a section called *For Further Reflection*. Sometimes the reflections will point out and explain specific ideas found within the psalm itself. At other times, I have in these reflections and questions used the psalms more freely to encourage various thoughts that may be helpful to you. Perhaps a particular personal memory. Or perhaps some reflection on where and with whom you are living and interacting now — and how you might, like the psalmist, live fully in this moment. At a given time, you may find some of the reflections more appropriate for your life than others. Some questions will have meaning today, others perhaps tomorrow. You will also notice that the book has purposely been designed in a spacious way so that you can, if you wish, make notes — of memories or of new thoughts and feelings — in the margins and in other blank spaces. This is *your* book, designed to address *you* on *your* life's journey.

The *Prayer* that follows the reflection summarizes and personalizes the messages of the explicated line or lines. This prayer, too, in its address to God, is intended to give voice to your own experience on your own life's journey. Each prayer will include the phrase, "Blessed are You, Adonai. . . ." *Adonai* is one of the many names for God in Hebrew, and is often understood as referring to the most merciful aspect of God's self. It is a name that suggests particular intimacy and will, I hope, encourage your own sense of deep closeness to God.

This book may be approached in many different ways. You might choose to read it from cover to cover, as one might read a novel. Or you can begin with whichever of the three psalms you choose, depending on your needs and interests at the moment. Psalm 121 is a psalm of journeying and pilgrimage. Psalm 23 is a psalm of rest and re-plenishment. Psalm 98 is a psalm of praise and exaltation. Which psalm best meets your needs now? Then, too, some readers will be more interested in the explanations of the psalms than in the reflections; others will be drawn to the prayers. On the first reading, you might decide to read only the prayers on a one-a-day basis. Whatever your approach, I hope you will use this book flexibly and creatively for your own best purposes. It is for *you* to decide how you will benefit from it the most today and tomorrow. I might add that while you may wish to read this book yourself, it can also be read *to* you by your husband or wife, your son or daughter, your friend or roommate, your rabbi or minister — whoever is your caregiver. Or it can be read to *groups* of your friends and fellow travelers. Wonderful conversations could ensue!

May the words of the psalms, the reflections, and the prayers bring you a profound inner peace and a sense of God's deep and abiding presence.

ACKNOWLEDGMENTS

In the fall of 2000 I told my friend Willem Mineur, Art Director at Eerdmans (and the designer of the cover for this book), that I had a number of ideas for a series of books. After a few minutes, Willem asked if I had met Jon Pott, Vice President and Editor-in-Chief at Eerdmans. I had not. Willem offered to speak to Jon about me. Shortly thereafter Jon and I met, and thus began a new friendship and a shared vision for this book. Jon encouraged me to write from my heart and to share the richness of Judaism and Christianity with an aging and searching audience. I had a vision, Jon had a number of suggestions for a direction, and we hope that this book will be helpful to many on their journey through aging. *The Lord Is My Shepherd: Psalms to Accompany Us on Our Journey through Aging* is the result of much writing and research, but, more importantly, it is the result of a deep and continuous religious and interpersonal dialogue between a committed Jew and a committed Christian who wanted to do more than "write a book." For his insights and caring critique — but mostly for his friendship — I will always be grateful to Jon Pott. My colleague and friend, Dr. Barry Bandstra of Hope College, graciously assisted me with the necessary Hebrew transliterations.

My wife, Dr. Shirley Kane Lewis, has been my closest friend and partner for forty years. She knows the difference between "writing words" and "writing truths." Each time she would read a revised manuscript she would skillfully and lovingly find the truths and show me where words were waiting for new life. I dedicate this book to her.

My daughters, Julie Devorah Torem and Jamie Suzanne Masco, have been constant sources of encouragement, as have my sons-in-law, Shachar and Tony. The fruits of their love, Max and Ellie and Troy, Joey, and Jake, are my foretaste of eternity.

I Lift My Eyes

אשא עיני

———∞———

PSALM 121

Psalm 121

1 I will lift up mine eyes unto the hills, from whence
   cometh my help.
2 My help cometh from the LORD, which made heaven
   and earth.
3 He will not suffer thy foot to be moved: he that
   keepeth thee will not slumber.
4 Behold, he that keepeth Israel shall neither slumber
   nor sleep.
5 The LORD is thy keeper: the LORD is thy shade upon
   thy right hand.
6 The sun shall not smite thee by day, nor the moon
   by night.
7 The LORD shall preserve thee from all evil: he shall
   preserve thy soul.
8 The LORD shall preserve thy going out and thy
   coming in from this time forth, and even for
   evermore.

Psalm 121

I lift my eyes unto the mountains,
(Asking) where will my help come from?

My help comes from (being with) Adonai,
Who makes heaven and earth.

He will not let your foot deviate from the right course:
Your guardian will not even become drowsy.

Of course, no slumber, no sleeping
Marks Israel's guardian.

Adonai is your guardian,
Adonai is your protection
At your right hand.

By day the sun will not strike you,
Nor the moon by night.

Adonai will guard you from all danger;
He will guard your soul.

Adonai will guard your going (out)
And your coming (in)
From this time and through eternity.

Psalm 121

INTRODUCTION

Psalm 121 is one of the so-called "pilgrim," or "traveler's," hymns, originally meant to reassure the pilgrim as he or she journeyed to or from a religious observance, most likely in Jerusalem. These psalms, numbers 120–134, are also called psalms of ascent, referring both physically and symbolically to an ascent of Mount Zion. Psalm 121 is a psalm of assurance that we are not alone, no matter where we are on our journey, and whether we are awake and fully conscious or asleep. The faithful God of Abraham, Isaac, and Jacob is with us even in our loneliest and most fearful moments. At the very beginning of the psalm the writer asks the question that is central to each of our lives: "I lift my eyes unto the mountains, Where will my help come from?" It is as though he is saying: "When I look up from my bed or my chair or wherever I am at this exact moment in my journey through life, where is the source of my help and reassurance?" Here, at the very beginning of the psalm, the psalmist offers immediate comfort. "My help comes from being with the Lord, the Maker of Heaven and Earth!"

The comforting message here is the solace of knowing and believing that the God who is capable of creating an entire world also knows and cares intimately about each of us.

The psalmist continues to tell us that though *we* may slumber and sleep, God is always awake and always vigilant on our behalf. In certain aspects, this psalm is a restatement of the blessing Aaron and his sons were to convey to the children of Israel according to Numbers 6:24-26:

> The LORD bless you and guard you.
> The LORD make His face to shine upon you,
> and be gracious unto you.
> The LORD lift up his countenance upon you
> and give you peace.

You are not alone, promises the psalmist. God will be beside you and journey with you, shielding you from all that may seem harmful.

As you read this psalm with the short meditations and prayers I have supplied, think about the journey of your own life, both past and present, and know that in your going out or your coming in, as the psalmist says, the Lord is by your side.

Psalm 121

I lift my eyes unto the mountains,
(Asking) where will my help come from?

At the very beginning of this psalm we are confronted by the numerous images mountains bring to mind. Do the mountains represent a place of safety and refuge from our enemies, as they often have for various peoples? Or are they foreboding and dangerous? In our own lives, we might ask, do the walls of our homes and rooms protect us, like the mountains, from lurking dangers and uncertainties? Or do they inspire fear and isolate us from the warmth and security of the life we used to know and love? Do the colors of the walls, the pictures, and memories offer us solace and hope? Do they bring the reassurance we want and need? Or do they overwhelm us with anxiety and seem to cut us off from what we can no longer have? To take the image in another way, must we see beyond our immediate daily surroundings and look to the lofty heights of the mountains? Do we need to look somewhere beyond ourselves? And if so, where and to whom?

On our journey through life, where do we see ourselves in relation to the mountains? Are we ascending, drawing closer to God, or are we descending and feeling estranged and distanced? In the biblical period, one of the names of God was *El Elyon,* "God of the most high." Some believed that God dwelled in the uppermost reaches of the mountains themselves, while others thought that God moved like a spirit between the high mountains and heaven itself. When we look up at the high mountains, we may be confronted with both hope and fear. But for the psalmist, fear is in the end overcome by hope and reassurance. That is God's promise.

Each day of our life may begin in a similar way: I open my eyes in the morning and I am keenly aware of the mountain-like obstacles and disabilities that confront me. What is the source of my help? Will my day be filled with fear and a sense of hopelessness? Or will I find in the mountains a sustaining hope and promise? Will God reach down to me as I journey to ascend on high? Will He enable me to see with my eyes and heart? Do I even want to be seen by God? By anyone at this time? Are there times when, because of bitterness or resentment or embarrassment, I just want to hide away from all those who surround me? And also from God?

One of the greatest obstacles to our sense of well-being is our deep feeling of diminishment and uselessness. We have been taught to worship at the shrine of youth. "Monotheism," the great twentieth-century Jewish scholar Rabbi Abraham Joshua Heschel once remarked, "has acquired a new meaning: the one and only thing that counts is being young" (*The Wisdom of Heschel*, 107). Appreciating the wisdom and holiness of age and of a life filled with experience, Rabbi Heschel argued against so simplistic a view. Instead, he would have had us see that youth is the anteroom ushering us into the wisdom and richness that can come only with age. Heschel devoted his life to teaching that a living, dynamic relationship between the individual and God exists at *every* stage in the journey of our lives, including the journey through aging.

FOR FURTHER REFLECTION

1. *What are your feelings when you are faced with a mountain of worry, and it feels like too much? How do you deal with this challenge? What are the things now that frustrate and anger you? Or embarrass you? That may make you want to lower your head and not see — or be seen by — anyone else? Including God.*

2. *Was there a person in your life, or is there one now, who could reassure you that what seemed like a mountain was really a series of smaller hills that together you could climb or go around?*

3. *Remember a time when someone you loved said: "I don't know how to handle this huge, mountain-like responsibility that is before me." What suggestions did you make and how did you help her regain perspective?*

4. *Think about the comfort you find in your present "surroundings." Talk about the security you feel in your room or home — surrounded by the mountain-like walls and guarded entrances and exits.*

5. *Do you think about your life as a journey, a pilgrimage, and what that means? That you came from somewhere and have*

the opportunity, also at this stage in your life, to travel purposefully toward something? Where did you come from, and in what ways — perhaps totally unexpected — has your past prepared you for where you are now? Where are you now? What meaningful opportunities still summon you, if you will but take care to see them?

6. Are you able to see opportunities at this place in your journey through life that you did not have when you were younger? More time to reflect and to take joy in what surrounds you? A greater wisdom than you once had? A richer body of experience? How might these help you in turn to help others?

7. An eighteenth-century Jewish maxim states: "Just as the hand held before the eye can hide the tallest mountain, so the routine of everyday life can keep you from seeing the vast radiance and secret wonders that fill the world." How might this statement apply to you?

———

PRAYER

Adonai, who dwells in the highest places and in the recesses of my heart, I call out to you. I ask that You be present and close to me as

I journey through this day. Sometimes I feel that a mountain looms before me, and I don't know (I cannot always see) if it is one of beauty and opportunity, or fear and loss. Like so many before me, I too ask: "Where or Who is the source of my help?" Encourage me to know in the deepest recesses of my heart and soul that You are my Help. Be at my side today and help me to know what is truly mountainous — and how I may — with Your assurance — overcome the fears and insecurities that are so much a part of me.

There were times in the past, even when I did not know it, that You were with me. Be with me, I pray, today. See me, and let me see You in my journey. Blessed are You, Adonai, who brings calm and reassurance to my day.

Psalm 121

**My help comes from (being with) Adonai,
Who makes heaven and earth**

In these words of the psalm, the questioner answers his own question! It is as though he reflects on the experiences of his life and says: "Wait a minute! *Adonai* has been with me throughout my life. Sometimes I could not see or feel the presence of Adonai, but He was there." The psalmist, speaking through the questioner, reminds us that a God who chooses to create both the Heavens and the Earth — and all that is contained within them — would certainly choose to help us, guide us, and encourage us. He would not abandon us now.

The Hebrew of this line is filled with wonderful possibilities. The word *maa-im* — usually not adequately translated in English versions — is understood in rabbinic Hebrew as "being with." The psalmist is telling us that whether we know it or not, God is with us. The rabbis tell a story about a young schoolboy in a traditional Cheder (one-room school) in Eastern Europe. During a particular lesson the rabbi posed the following to his students: "If you can tell me where God is, I will give you a shiny silver coin." One of the more reflective students turned to the rabbi and said: "If you can tell me where God is *not,* I will give you two shiny coins!"

How often have we thought or heard someone else ask, "How did I ever get to this God-forsaken place or time in my life?" The story of the young student helps us to understand that there is no time or place without God. Everything and everyone is infused with God. Sometimes we just don't know it, or have to be reminded.

Rabbi Lawrence Kushner, a gifted writer and mystic, has devoted an entire book to the story of Jacob and his dream of a ladder and to the Hebrew phrase, "God was in this place and I, I did not know." Jacob, you may remember, was the son of Isaac and Rebekah and the twin brother of Esau. Jacob had earlier stolen his brother Esau's birthright, and, with his mother's help, had manipulated Isaac, his father, into giving him the blessing reserved for the firstborn, Esau. Now, somewhere between Beersheva and Haran, Jacob is fleeing from Esau and perhaps from much of his former self. He dreams of a ladder with angels ascending and descending. He receives an assurance from the God of Abraham and Isaac that he will not be alone on his journey and that his children will inherit the land on which he lies and even much of that on which he will travel. At the end of his dream (Genesis 28:16), Jacob utters the phrase, "God was in this place and I, I did not know it." Rabbi Kushner tells us that when the mystics read the phrase "and I, I did not know it," they struggled to understand why Jacob would not know that God was in that place. Studying the phrase "I, I. . ." they concluded that Jacob could not experience God because he was too full of *himself.*

Sometimes in our journey through aging we may be totally preoccupied with ourselves. We refuse to see beyond our own disabilities, pains, and diminished capacities. We become consumed with "my pain," "I want," and "if only." Regret exhausts our energies and we are unable or unwilling to see God and "the other." Perhaps we should ask ourselves a series of different questions: Am I truly open to God and to my value in God's sight? To the possibilities, perhaps even the special possibilities now, for meaning and joy in life? Am *I* the only one who feels pain, loneliness, frustration, limitations? Do I dare move beyond my depression and doubt and to reach out — to my roommate, friend, caregiver, family? Can I make my *I* a little smaller and theirs a little larger and richer?

The psalmist reminds us that when we open ourselves up, Adonai is there — waiting and wanting to be with us. In Hebrew, *Adonai* refers to God in His most merciful aspect, and day after day God creates and cares, cares and creates. In our rooms, walking beside our walkers, in our bed and at our table, and in our neighbors — in all these places, God, the Maker of Heaven and Earth, is there.

FOR FURTHER REFLECTION

1. *Have there been times in your life when God was present and you did not know it? What can block your sense of God's presence? Try to recall a time when you sensed God's presence, but you were too full of yourself or too involved in the "stuff of life" to listen. What happened as a result of your not being available? What did you miss? Who missed you?*

2. *Think of a person, past or present, who stepped into your life and helped you to use all your senses to discover the wholeness of the world — and of yourself. Who taught you about the importance of the "other"?*

3. *Do you ever think about the cares and needs of the person who is now your caregiver? What do you know of his or her journey?*

PRAYER

Adonai, who creates and cares and cares and creates again, I do know that You are here for me and that I can be here for others. In the creation of the Earth You formed me in Your image with the capacity for wisdom and justice. You gave me five senses so that I might see and hear and feel, even taste and smell the wonders of Your world. When I can step back from the doubt and pain that is part of my life; when I can empty myself of some of the pettiness and real loss that creeps into my life, I discover and rediscover You!

In the scent of spring and warm food; in the touch of a caring hand; from my window seeing the pure white clouds float gently across an unending sky; in music and words of healing, and in the sweet or pungent tastes of foods, I open again to You. Day after day You renew the world and all that is within it. I know, then, that day after day You renew me. Help me this day to see and rejoice in my renewal to share it with others through my journey with You. Blessed are You, Adonai, who daily renews life in my inner most world.

He will not let your foot deviate from the right course:
Your guardian will not even become drowsy

Of course, no slumber, no sleeping
Marks Israel's guardian

The opening lines of the Hebrew text have a wonderfully reassuring resonance:

> *Al-yitaan lamot raglecha*
> *Al-yanum shomerecha*

It sounds like the comforting whisper of a parent or an older brother or sister into the ear of a younger child. The word that is often translated "stumble" can mean "to trip." It can also be translated as "to deviate from the right course."

What a beautiful image! God who dwells in the highest and lowliest of reaches is with us each step of our way. If we choose to stay open and receptive to Him, He will not let us stray from the right path. Though we may momentarily stumble or stray, He will be with us and not let us fall or lose our way.

Today, many corporations take their executives on "trusting walks" and challenging ropes courses, forcing members to rely on one another and to build trust. Father Henri Nouwen, the well-known Catholic priest, was fascinated by circus aerialists. One year, while visiting his native Holland, he took his father to the circus. When the aerialists came out, Henri was glued to his seat. What feats they performed! How amazed he was with their breathtaking skill! After the show, Father Nouwen talked with one of the aerialists and complimented him for his special gifts of timing and dexterity — the way he tumbled and flew through the air, only to be caught by his partner on the other trapeze at precisely the right second. The tumbler then turned to Father Nouwen and remarked that his *real* gift was the gift of faith — faith that the other aerialist would be there at the exact moment he needed to be caught. God, the psalmist is reassuring us, is there at that exact moment of our need, but we have to dare to believe. We must extend our hand and heart toward His.

This infinitely caring God is a God who requires no sleep; He is eternally vigilant. The Hebrew text may be understood as "your guardian will not slumber" or as "your guardian will not even become drowsy" — because you are simply too important in God's world! Twenty-four hours a day, day after day, year after year, generation after generation — God watches and cares and guides us on our way.

Like a father, He also *delights* in us. Sometimes my daughter will call and ask me to baby-sit one of my grand-sons. The youngest, Jacob, is only two years old. I always make sure to rest on the day before I go to baby-sit him — not just because he demands so much of my energy, but also because I love him so much I don't want to miss any-thing. I want to experience every move, every new word, and each happening in Jacob's life. Even when *he* naps, *I* am attuned to his stirrings and breathing. That's how God feels about each of us. Not only does He guide and protect us, He *delights* in us and wants to see our every move!

FOR FURTHER REFLECTION

1. *As we grow older — perhaps now needing to rely on a walker or on the steady hand of a son or a daughter or a nurse's aide — we become especially aware of the dangers of stumbling. But we can stumble in other ways as well. What are the particular threats to your well-being now?*

2. *Do you resent needing the help of others? Do you find it hard to trust? What are some of the positive gifts of accepting our neediness and learning to trust? Of taking joy in the gifts that others can give to us? What gift in turn does your relationship of trust allow you to give to the person you trust?*

3. *Who, when you were young, made you feel very special and very important? Think about that person. What you would like to say to him or her now? Who makes you feel special today?*

4. *Can you recall a time when you stayed up all night with a child? How do you feel when you have a sleepless night? What thoughts, pains, and feelings keep you awake?*

5. *If you could describe the most wonderful experience you ever had of being watched over and cared for, what would it be?*

6. *Did you ever feel delighted in when you had the full attention*

of your parents or grandparents? Or your husband or wife or best friend?

7. *Do you ever feel not only watched over but also delighted in by God?*

〜〜〜

PRAYER

Adonai, so often I am unsure of my way and I doubt both my direction and determination. Sometimes I even lie sleepless, clothed in worry and fear. I am afraid that I might fall and hurt myself, or that something might befall me. Help me to feel sure that even when I am sleepless You are awake, choosing neither to slumber nor sleep as You watch over me. In my stillness grant me the rest that my body and soul need so that I might experience the world and its wonders as fully as possible. As children are calmed when they say: "Now I lay me down to sleep, I pray the Lord my soul to keep," help me to be calmed by the assurance that even when I am old, You guide and guard my soul; that the nourishment of rest and inner peace is the gift You willingly give to me. Guide me through the day with a sure step. And help me to know that if I nap during the day, You smile and say: "Rest, my beloved, I am

here with you." Blessed are You, Adonai, who delights in me and
guides and guards me at all times.

Adonai is your guardian,
Adonai is your protection
At your right hand

Sometimes I wonder what it would be like to be a famous
public figure with my own bodyguard. I imagine a very
muscular and commanding person whose total responsi-
bility would be to make sure that no harm would come to
me. This person would protect me from enemies but also
from the thousands of people who just want to get close
enough to see me or to touch me (remember, I said this
was my imagination!). And then I remember that in God's
eyes, we are all famous and notable and beloved. The
writer of the ancient book of wisdom called *Sirach* taught
us this when he wrote: "Let us now praise famous men,

and our fathers that begot us" (44:1). He reminds us that each member of each generation *is* famous and of ultimate worth in God's eyes.

The Hebrew Bible has many different names for God, and, as we have seen, Adonai is the name most often associated with the most merciful aspects of God. In Hebrew the word for "mercy" is derived from that for "womb." When we use the term *Adonai* for God we are referring to the nurturing, enveloping, maternal way in which God *always* cares for us. The word *zal,* often translated "protection," is also the word for "shade" in Hebrew. In other words, Adonai guards us and shades us from the heat and harm that may surround us. Adonai, the psalmist reminds us, is as close as our right hand.

FOR FURTHER REFLECTION

1. *As you look over the span of your life, who were some of the people who stood up for you when you needed it? Who guarded and protected you?*

2. *What are your most immediate fears today? A roommate who is difficult and unfriendly? A nurse who is short-tempered and unhelpful? The medical tests you must have tomorrow? A loss of control and independence?*

3. *Who stands up for you today? Is there a person who helps you to know that he or she is right there for you? To whom do you reach out?*

4. *How does it feel to accept care today? How does it feel to give it? Can you accept care and retain your dignity at the same time?*

5. *Can you be God's merciful and protective hand to someone else? For whom can you be the "right hand" — family, roommate, nurse's aide?*

⎯⎯⎯ ⧜ ⎯⎯⎯

PRAYER

Adonai, I do know that You are with me. You are the One who guards me from dangers I cannot even fathom, and Who protects me even when I do not know that I need protection. For the prophet Jonah You prepared a wonderful shade plant as protection from the harsh sun. You provided shelter and safety to the generations that came before me, and I pray You will do so for those who come after me. Help me today to draw closer to You and to feel your presence more closely. I do want to feel You as closely as I feel my right hand. Hold my fragile and vulnerable hand in Yours and journey with me today. Help me to feel and enjoy your protection in all the waking and sleeping moments of my day and night. Blessed are You, Adonai, who holds me ever so gently in Your hand.

Psalm 121

By day the sun will not strike you,
Nor the moon by night

In the book of Genesis we are told about the creation of the world; we learn that on the fourth day the moon and sun were created (1:16). The sun, the greater celestial body, was created to rule by day, and the lesser moon by night. The ancients, including the Hebrews, believed that each of these heavenly spheres had magical powers.

We can well imagine how awesome these two bodies seemed to the ancients when we think of the desert-like regions in which only the moon and stars can be seen at night. And when we consider the overpowering and unforgiving heat of the sun during the desert day.

In these short lines, the psalmist is telling us that while there are people who believe in the godlike power of the sun or the moon, he believes in the power of the One who created these spheres and who ultimately controls them. God, the creator and power behind these heavenly bodies, is also the One who interacts and gives power and meaning to our lives. God has made you a promise, says the psalmist. He will control the sun so that it does not exhaust you during the day. He will teach you how to protect yourself from its harm, and also how to appreciate its warmth and benefit from its wonderful energy.

God will protect you in the night as well. The moon may be seen to symbolize the bitter cold of the night. Or, as often in literature, it may represent some frightening and evil influence. The psalmist reassures us we will not become moonstruck (recall the word "lunatic") or threatened by other fears that may be inspired in us by the moods of the moon. You do not have to fear the dark and quiet of night. And you do not need to fear what may seem a nighttime in your own mind and soul. Commenting on this psalm and its meaning for our own daily walk in life, the Christian biblical scholar Leslie C. Allen notes:

> As the believer walks in step with the rhythms which make up daily life and represent the providential ordering of human existence, he may do so with the assurance that God is with him in his daily toil and rest, ever helping and protecting. . . . The potent promise, "I will be with you," avails not only for heroes of the faith such as a Moses or Joshua, but passes in turn to ordinary believers. (*Word Biblical Commentary,* vol. 21, p. 154)

Sometimes as we age we feel that much of our life is out of control. The psalmist is reassuring us that God *is* in control of the cosmos as well as the intimate complexities of our life. That is the promise God made to each of us without condition.

FOR FURTHER REFLECTION

1. *Think about the picture in this psalm of the blazing sun. What are some of the things that make you feel especially threatened and exposed during the day? Do you worry about having to do certain things under the "full glare" of other people's attention? Do you worry about very publicly embarrassing yourself because you can no longer walk or eat properly? Do you sometimes feel that you have lost all your privacy? Do you hate to be bathed by someone else? Do you feel vulnerable and exposed? How might you still see yourself shaded by a loving and protective God?*

2. *Can you also appreciate the wonderful warmth and light of the sun, perhaps in the way it lights up the courtyard outside your window? Or the particular way it throws its beams gloriously across your room? Can you take joy in its flirtation as it hides behind a cloud?*

3. *Close your eyes and imagine for a moment that you are on a beach and that it is a perfect summer's day. Write or talk about how it feels to have the warmth of the sun over your shoulder. Are you sitting alone, with another person or with a*

*group? Who are the members of your group? What special peo-
ple would you like to sit with today? How do you feel when
the light comes brightly into your life?*

4. *Do you sometimes have difficulty sleeping at night? Do your
worries come mainly then, when all is silent and when, per-
haps, all outside your window is awash in the eerie light of the
moon? Can your problems seem overwhelming when you are
so alone with them? Are you really alone? Is this an especially
good time to be open to the Lord who made Heaven and Earth?*

5. *If you are honest, do you worry deep down about losing some
of your mental capacity as you grow older? About losing your
memory? Think about God's promise not to abandon you in
whatever may seem to be night for you.*

6. *Consider the moon in another way. Does the full light of the
moon ever fill you with a lovely yearning? For what? Here are
four lines from Samuel Taylor Coleridge's great poem "The
Rime of the Ancient Mariner," which you may remember from
your days in school: "The moving Moon went up the sky,/And
nowhere did abide:/Softly she was going up,/And a star or two
beside. . . ." Why are these lines so lovely? Do they mysteri-
ously hint at a world somehow beyond? Do they give you any
sense of an eternity?*

PRAYER

Adonai, who created the day and night, who separated them with the sun and the moon, You know that sometimes I struggle with the thoughts and memories that invade the calm of my day and night. Sometimes sleep eludes me and past and present become blurred in nightmarish dreams. At other times I feel that tiredness consumes me. Help me, I pray, to find the solace and calm my body and soul truly need. When I arise in the morning, give me the courage to face the day as I would face the warmth and light of the sun; with the guarded optimism brought to me by age and experience. When the days are gloomy, lead me to Your light within and brighten my way as I recall the spring and summer of life and the beauty of autumn. Let the moon be Your beacon in the uncertainty of my night and sleep; the assurance that You will be with me tomorrow, also. Blessed are You, Adonai, who reassures me throughout the days and nights of my life.

Adonai will guard you from all danger;
He will guard your soul

In these lines the psalmist is telling us that he is conclud-
ing his promise that God is with us; guiding and guard-
ing, ever vigilant, day or night. He is inviting us to go back
over each line of this beautiful psalm and, with him, to ar-
rive at the conclusion that Adonai has been with us from
the very beginning of our lives, and that He is with us now
and always. It is as though the psalmist has said, "God has
given you a lifetime-plus guarantee, and I am simply tell-
ing you that He is carrying through!" Life doesn't get any
better that that!

The Hebrew word *nefesh* is often translated as "life,"
but is more accurately understood as "soul." It is derived
from a verb used in Hebrew liturgy to describe the way in
which God, after the creation of the world, rested and re-
vitalized His soul. This suggests that God is guarding
our soul — which is our life and much more. The soul, I
believe, is the divine spark that is given to each of us and
is the godly flame within. It kindles, burns, and is radi-
ant with light and warmth and is nurtured at every mo-

ment by God. It, like God's guidance and guardianship, is eternal.

FOR FURTHER REFLECTION

1. *The psalmist promises us that God will guard us from all danger — dangers that we anticipate and dangers we cannot possibly expect. What was the greatest danger you ever faced, and how did you survive it? What is the greatest danger in your life today and how do you cope with it? What dangers do you fear as you age?*

2. *A Jewish maxim states: "Though the world is full of trouble, each man [and woman] feels only his own." How do you understand these words? How true are they to your experience?*

3. *Who in addition to God guards and protects you?*

4. *In times of doubt and despair many people turn to friends and family, as well as to God. To whom do you turn? Who turns to you?*

5. *The psalmist has told us that God will guard our soul. How do you understand the concept of "soul" and what are some of the ways in which you nourish your soul?*

6. *Do you pray daily? For what and for whom do you pray? Do you include the needs of others in your prayer? Do you express gratitude in your prayer?*

PRAYER

Adonai, it is so easy for me to slip into moments and sometimes days of despair and doubt. How many times have I asked: "Where is my help and when will it come?" I know You are here with me. You guard not only my physical being, but my spiritual being also. I want so much to see how today and every day You will guard my life. I do know that there will be times when I will be challenged by life, and that I will need to choose to accept the challenge directly, or to absorb it in a way that I can best tolerate. Like the psalmist who wrote this beautiful piece, I am reassured that You will guard me now and forever. You guard my "life" and all that it encompasses; from its very opening sentence to the conclusion that You have willed. And I am at peace. Blessed are You, Adonai, who has placed the spark of life within me.

Adonai will guard your going (out)
And your coming (in)
From this time and through eternity

In Hebrew liturgy, this line would be called the *Chatimah*, the conclusion. Remember the question posed at the very beginning of the psalm — "Where will my help come from?" The Hebrew here is absolutely simple in its construction and meter. *Adonai yishmor tsaatecha uvo-echa . . . maa-atah ve-ad-olam.* To those who understand Hebrew, this feels and has the tonal quality we expect at the culmination of a great symphony.

Not only is the question asked at the beginning of the psalm firmly answered; a greater promise is given. God will guard you in your every move, your going out and your coming in, not only in this time of your life but forever. In its purest form the Hebrew text tells us that the promise is "good" from this very moment in time through all that we understand as eternity.

The Hebrew phrase *maa-atah ve-ad-olam* truly means much more than the simple translation "from now and through Eternity." *Olam* is often translated as "universe"

— as in, "Blessed are you, Adonai, King of the Universe." The rabbis have interpreted *olam* to refer to much more than the known and as yet unknown universe. It refers to all that will ever be or be known. It is truly a future beyond time and space. God's promise is to guard us now and into that timeless and endless *olam*. The awesome mountain (mentioned in the very first line) may tumble and become no more than dust and rubble, but God's promise of guarding and protecting will endure beyond time.

We often think of mountains as timeless and everlasting, but compared to the promise of eternity and God's surety — the God who is our immovable rock — the mountain is little more than dust blowing in the wind, and *we*, because of the soul within us, are immortal and always protected. The reassurance has been given, and in this psalm the promise of Deuteronomy 28:6-7 has been reaffirmed:

Blessed shall you be when you come in, and blessed shall you be when you go out. Adonai will cause your enemies who rise up against you to be smitten before you. They shall come out against you one way, and shall flee before you in seven ways.

The pilgrim who has come to Jerusalem, the earthly City of God, is assured that as he was cared for in this stage of life, so he will also be cared for beyond the now — and even beyond the future.

FOR FURTHER REFLECTION

1. *Throughout your life many people have talked about "eternity." How would you explain eternity in your own words? If you could live for an eternity, would you do it? Why or why not?*

2. *You have been promised that God will guard you wherever you are on your faith journey. Talk or write about where you are on this important journey, and where you might like to be. Has your faith journey taken you where you thought it would? How has your journey taken you to new heights and depths?*

3. *God does not exempt any of us from the messiness of life. But He does guard us, letting us know that we are not alone — not abandoned. Do you feel God in your life today? Are you willing to reach out so that God may come in?*

4. *What does this poem, written by an anonymous poet in the sixteenth century, mean to you?*

> *God be in my head*
> *And in my understanding;*

Psalm 121

> *God be in my eyes*
> *And in my looking;*

> *God be in my mouth*
> *And in my speaking;*

> *God be in my heart*
> *And in my thinking;*

> *God be at my end*
> *And at my departing.*

5. *Judaism and Christianity teach us that the soul is eternal. What does "eternity of the soul" mean to you and does it offer you comfort?*

PRAYER

Adonai, You have given me the gifts of life and of protection from all fears. And while you guard and protect me in this life, You have also promised me that there is more! The mountains may crumble and the seas may become dry land, but the soul that You have planted within me will live in eternity beyond time and space.

With certainty, I can now say and believe: "I lift my eyes to the highest mountains and I need not fear the high places or the walls that surround me. They can be another source of comfort. I turn my eyes again to the very depths of the seas, and I need not fear the lowest of places, for You are there. Wherever I am and whenever I am — You are with me!" And my heart and soul are calm again. Blessed are You, Adonai, who has given me life and love without end.

Adonai Is My Shepherd

יהוה רעי

———— ∞∞ ————

PSALM 23

Psalm 23

1 The LORD is my shepherd; I shall not want.

2 He maketh me to lie down in green pastures: he
leadeth me beside the still waters.

3 He restoreth my soul: he leadeth me in the paths of
righteousness for his name's sake.

4 Yea, though I walk through the valley of the shadow
of death, I will fear no evil: for thou art with me;
thy rod and thy staff they comfort me.

5 Thou preparest a table before me in the presence of
mine enemies: thou anointest my head with oil; my
cup runneth over.

6 Surely goodness and mercy shall follow me all the
days of my life: and I will dwell in the house of the
LORD for ever.

Psalm 23

Adonai is my shepherd;
I shall not lack.
In well-suited meadows
He will make it possible for me to lie down;
Near restful waters He will guide me.
He will restore my soul.
He will lead me along paths of righteousness
    for His own purposes.
Even though I shall walk in the valley of death's
    shadow, I shall fear no evil, for
You are with me;
Your spear and Your staff, they will give me comfort.
You will prepare a table for me in front of my enemies,
You have anointed my head with oil,
My cup is satisfaction.
Surely goodness and unconditional love will pursue me
    all the days of my life,
And I will dwell in the house of Adonai for days
    without end.

Psalm 23

INTRODUCTION

The 23rd psalm is by far the most familiar of all the psalms. It has become an integral part of life-cycle ceremonies in both the Jewish and Christian communities, often recited as a central piece at weddings, anniversary celebrations, and funeral and memorial services. This psalm has also become an integral part of daily and weekly worship celebrations.

If Psalm 121 is a psalm of movement, Psalm 23 is a psalm of rest. And if the images of Psalm 121 are of lofty — and perhaps dangerous — hills or mountains and of arduous and rocky paths where we might stumble or lose our way in our journey through life, the setting of Psalm 23 is lush and pastoral and is quietly replenishing to our souls. The mighty God who in Psalm 121 is our protector from above is now the tender shepherd intimately and protectively beside us.

Psalm 23 is a psalm of deep confidence that begins with the affirmation that "The Lord (Adonai) *is* my shepherd" and concludes with the declaration "And I shall dwell in the house of the Lord (Adonai) forever." While there are many names for God in the Hebrew Bible, the name *Adonai* refers, as we have seen, especially to God's mercy and lovingkindness.

Though we do not truly know who wrote this psalm, it is often ascribed to King David. And in fact, whoever the author was, the imagery of the psalm, while pastoral, may also, in its reference to anointing and its suggestion of a royal banquet, be seen as kingly. In the ancient world, a king was often thought of as the shepherd of his people.

The psalm is written in a manner which suggests that the author was an older person who had experienced much of life; one who had known that physical and emotional distress and enemies, as well as death, are real. And yet, the writer reassures us, these adversaries ultimately cannot hurt us or diminish us because, as we are told in beautiful poetic and visual detail, God is always with us. Our relationship with God is certain from the very beginning of life to the life beyond. We are assured that our souls will constantly be restored; that we will be guided in straight paths and that goodness and mercy *shall* follow and be with us — always.

Read this beautiful psalm and its commentaries through the eyes of its writer and give yourself the gift of reflecting on your own physical, emotional, and spiritual journey through life.

Psalm 23

Adonai is my shepherd

In Hebrew liturgy, prayers that begin with the term *Adonai* are understood to be deeply personal and intimate. Sometimes, they are even uttered with a whisper, as one would share a secret or longing with the closest of friends. The 23rd psalm is an invitation to intimacy between the merciful God and the reader. The psalmist writes in a way that makes this intimacy perfectly clear. The Lord is a shepherd, with all the close and tender care this role implies. But further, Adonai is *my* shepherd, not *our* shepherd. In other words, *I* have a special relationship with Adonai! In fact, in the New Testament the good shepherd is pictured as one who will seek out even the one sheep who has wandered from the fold. And in a significant reversal of what Israel had been warned would come from their having a king — that a king would take all the goods that they had (1 Samuel 8:10-13) — here is a shepherd-king who instead is at the service of each member of his flock. And our response can only be gratitude.

Theologian Walter Brueggemann notes that,

> In some other contexts (as in the lament of Psalm 77), the repeated reference to self sounds like an unhealthy obsession. But here that is not the case. Here the "I" statements are filled with gratitude, yielding, trust, and thanksgiving. The "I" here knows that in every case, life is fully cared for and resolved by this thou [God], who responds to and anticipates every need. . . . It is God's companionship that transforms every situation. It does not mean there are no deathly valleys, no enemies. But they are not capable of hurt, and so the powerful loyalty and solidarity of Yahweh (Adonai) comfort precisely in situations of threat. (155-56)

When Moses encountered God at the burning bush, as Rabbi Lawrence Kushner reminds us, he asked for God's name. And God responded *"Ehyeh Asher Ehyeh"* — often translated as "I will be what I will be" (Exodus 3:14). Kushner notes that in Hebrew there is no future tense of the verb. There is a past, a present, and an "imperfect." While the imperfect is often translated as future, it can also mean ever-changing and "not yet." What this suggests for our understanding of Psalm 23 is a God who is constantly, yet ever flexibly, available in His faithfulness to us.

In other parts of the Bible, God may be referred to as a warrior (Exodus 2:25 and Revelation 19:11) and often as a judge (Psalm 96 and Luke 18:6). But here we are given the image of a guiding and purposeful shepherd, one who helps us move along the path of life on our journey from birth to death. Here we also see our own yearning to be shepherded or guided by One in whom we place ultimate trust, and in whom we find our nurture and our direction in life. A rabbinic insight informs us "When the Shepherd blunders, his flock blunders after him" (Midrash, Deuteronomy Rabbah, 1:10). The Shepherd who leads and guides us does not blunder, and we can be comforted by his constant presence.

FOR FURTHER REFLECTION

1. *In what ways do you feel God leading or not leading you today? Can you feel God's guidance as you use your walker and receive help from your caregivers? Do you feel faithfully watched over as you take a refreshing and life-giving nap?*

2. *What are the attributes of a good shepherd? Who is a shepherd in your life today?*

3. *What are some of the ways in which you have shepherded others (family, friends, and neighbors)?*

4. *Can you remember which of your own shepherding and guiding experiences has brought you the greatest satisfaction? Which were the most disappointing?*

5. *What are the greatest challenges to your own faithfulness in being a shepherd to others?*

PRAYER

Adonai, there have been times when I have felt alone here and that no one cared. All of us have such moments; maybe even days.

Yet I know that even in my darkest moments, You, O Lord, are with me. In the healing, in the calm, the reaching out of family, friends, and caregivers, and in my choice to move toward hope, You have shepherded me. Wherever I have been, even in anger, pain, and doubt, Lord, You have been with me. As a shepherd guides his flock in caring and protective ways — even though the one who is shepherded may not understand the shepherd's plan — so are You, Adonai, my shepherd.

Throughout my life there have been times when I have felt this caring-mercy, and times when I have felt distanced from it. I pray that You will help me to feel it in each day of my life and to share the security and serenity it brings with others. Blessed are You, Adonai, creator of justice and mercy.

I shall not lack

The phrase *lo echsar* in the Hebrew text of Psalm 23 is most accurately translated as "I shall not lack." To lack means here much more than what we ordinarily mean by "want." In this psalm it means to be without something that is essential to life itself. And the psalmist, as he whispers to God, is saying: "Because You are God, I have not lacked what I most deeply need — and I will not lack. My trust is in You!"

A number of years ago my neighbor was walking with his young son in one of the local malls. When they came to a toy store, the son turned to his father and said: "Dad, I really *need* that airplane in the window." The father, seizing the chance to help his son understand the difference between wants and needs, said: "Jimmy, a need is something you absolutely have to have in your life. A want is something that might make your life more enjoyable but is not essential." They walked by a few more stores and Jimmy turned to his father and said: "I've been thinking about what you said, Dad, and I really *need* that airplane." That day the message did not get through. But today Jim is an ordained minister and clearly knows the difference between want and need.

Walter Brueggemann helps us to further understand the meaning of "to lack," particularly as it applies to Israelite society and Jewish memory:

The satisfaction of lacks can be appreciated in an Israelite context if the psalm is related to the meaning of Israel's memory. In Exod. 16:18 it is precisely manna, the surprising bread of heaven, that is the resolution of hunger, so that no one lacks. And in Deut. 2:7 the entire wilderness tradition is seen as a story in which there were no lacks, because God's steadfastness and goodness (cf. Ps. 23:6) [are] found adequate in the face of every threat to life. This psalm can recall situations of threat, but the poet knows that the powerful solidarity of God (Adonai) more than overrides the threat. The whole memory of Israel presses the psalmist toward trust. (*The Message of the Psalms,* 155)

All relationships of meaning, says the psalmist, are built on the foundation of trust *and genuine need.* Love, marriage, parenthood, friendship, interdependence, and the true sharing of time and space — all are built on this foundation. Rabbi Abraham Joshua Heschel reminds us:

Man is more than what he is to himself. In his reason he may be limited, in his will he may be wicked, yet he stands in a relation to God which he may betray but not sever, and which constitutes the essential meaning of his life. He is the knot in which heaven and earth are interlaced. (*Wisdom,* 20)

FOR FURTHER REFLECTION

1. *Think of a time in your youth when you wanted something so badly that you would have done almost anything for it. What was it? Share your story and enjoy its flavor. Age can offer us greater wisdom and discernment; it can also make us live in a smaller social and physical world — perhaps especially so in an assisted-care facility. What are your essential wants and needs today? Can you distinguish between them? Do you sometimes confuse them and become petty over small things?*

2. *Remember a time when you helped another (a family member, a friend, a coworker) to achieve something that was essential and lacking in that person's life. How did that feel? Have you done so recently?*

3. *What genuine need is not being adequately addressed in your life? Is there someone you can talk to about it?*

4. *Are there lacks in those around you that you should fill? Perhaps even by thanking someone for filling one of your needs?*

5. *Logan Pearsall Smith wrote, "There are two things to aim at in life: first to get what you want; and, after that, to enjoy it. Only the wisest of mankind achieve the second." How do you understand this comment in your life and surroundings? In the life of those around you?*

———⊗⊗⊗———

PRAYER

Adonai, it is so easy to confuse "want" and "need." As I look at my life and all the experiences it has brought me, I do see that You, O Lord, have understood my wants and needs. Food, clothing, shelter, a caring family and caregivers, You have provided for me. Though I may not have always understood, I have lacked for nothing! I may wish for the body or mind of youth, but my basic needs are addressed. In Your Love, You see that in the important aspects of my life, I shall not lack. You have taught me too, that all people want dignity and respect and to be acknowledged each day (see Matthew 6:7-13).

I know, too, that there are those who lack even a morsel of bread or a place in which to eat it. Be with them, O God of Mercy and Justice. Blessed are You, Adonai, who daily knows my every need.

In well-suited meadows
He will make it possible for me to lie down

In the Hebrew text, the phrase *binot deshe* means more than "green meadows," however comforting even this image is. In its most basic sense the phrase refers to something that is "handsome" or "well suited." The psalmist is telling us that we are given an abundance of all that is lovely and deeply suited to our nourishment in this life and the next. And here "green" is much more than a color; it is a reference to the richness and nourishing plentitude of life. This bounty and fullness reminds us of the Garden of Eden and of our relationship with God all the way back to Adam and Eve: "And God said: 'Let the Earth put forth grass, herb yielding seed, and fruit tree bearing fruit after its kind (wherein is the seed thereof, after its kind; and God saw that it was good)" (Genesis 1:11).

The verb *yarbeetsaanee* is most accurately translated as "He (God) will prepare (or make it possible for) me to lie down." We can lie down content because we have been so richly satisfied, and feel secure because our shepherd watches over us as we journey through life and beyond. If we look forward to the end of this psalm, we can even see our lying down in green pastures to refer to the time of our death, when, too, our shepherd will not desert us.

FOR FURTHER REFLECTION

1. *Did you ever lie in the plush green fields of summer or in a pile of freshly mown hay? What was that like? What today*

would give you the feeling of being enveloped in love and care? Who can show it to you best?

2. The Talmud states: "Three things soften a mans heart: a pleasant melody, a pleasant scene, and a fragrant odor" (Berakoth, 57b). What does this mean to you as you think of lying down in green meadows?

3. In our old age, most of us lie down much more than we once did. Rather than see this as a loss, how might you find contentment or joy in this? By opening yourself up more to quiet contemplation? By luxuriating in the beauty and plentitude of God's creation? Can you describe the scent of the flower in your room? Do you take time to surround yourself with great music, which is also a nourishing gift from God?

4. Do you have a compulsive need just to be busy? Do you find it difficult to "let go" and allow yourself to be nourished by the gifts of others?

5. In what ways has it been "made possible" for you now to lie down and to enjoy peace and contentment and the opportunity for enriching reflection and refreshing sleep? Whom should you thank?

6. It is wonderful to think that we may be given not necessarily what we would like, but what is "richly suited" to us. Can

you think of times in your life when you discovered that you were given a much richer gift than the thing you thought you wanted? How might this be true today as well?

7. Many of your family and friends now lie in the bosom of earth's green pastures. How did you first experience death in your family? Were you included in the necessary mourning? As you reflect today on your life, how do you want to be remembered?

————— ❧ —————

PRAYER

Adonai, I know that green is more than a color, it is a sign of life. It reminds me of the richness and hopeful nature of life. Throughout my life, You have helped me, Adonai, to make decisions that have enriched my life. I know, too, that I have made some decisions that have taken me away from the richness of Your green pastures and into places that appeared barren: but that is in the past. And one day, just as You have led me in this life, I pray You will gently lead me into the green pastures to be gathered with those who have preceded me in life and death. There, too, I know You will be with me.

Together we have journeyed through so many pastures, Lord, and each of them different; each for a different need and time in my life. When I approach the green meadows that You have already prepared for me, I pray that You will help me to know Your presence and to be reassured by Your comforting care. When I lie down in the bosom of Your Earth, I pray that You will continue to guide and guard my soul. Blessed are You, Adonai, who has placed eternal life within me.

Psalm 23

Near restful waters He will guide me

The still waters here promise to quench our thirst. But they also promise rest. Those who are familiar with great lakes and seas know well the unpredictable nature of the waters. From moment to moment they may change dramatically and dangerously. Without warning, as in the story of Jonah, they may alter from calm to turbulence. The tranquil afternoon sail may turn into a life-threatening squall, and we may find ourselves swallowed up in dangerous seas. Like the sailors who accompanied Jonah, we too look for and want to be guided to the tranquil waters.

In the Hebrew text of Psalm 23, the phrase *al maa menuchot* may be translated as "upon tranquil or restful waters." One of the words is used in Numbers 10:33 to refer to the resting place for the Ark of the Covenant and the people of Israel. The verb *nahal* — meaning guidance — also appears in Exodus 15:13, referring to the caring way in which God, for His own reasons and joy, guided and led the People of Israel out of Egypt, away from a place of turbulence and insecurity to a place of sufficiency flowing with milk and honey. It is that guidance and sufficiency which the psalmist here offers to each of us. He shares his personal faith with us, "a faith which draws on a rich treasury of personal experience" (Davidson, *The Vitality of Worship,* 84). I believe each of us has that treasury within us.

FOR FURTHER REFLECTION

1. *What are your doubts today that make you feel troubled and especially upset? And what do you need to help you find the still waters?*

2. *What is there in your own remembered "rich treasury of personal experience" that your faith can draw on for peace and restoration? Recall a time when you felt absolute calm, as though surrounded by the "still waters." Talk or think about this special time and place. Was there someone with you? When and where do you feel that absolute calm today? Is there a memory that helps you reach that calm? Perhaps of a hymn or another piece of music that can speak quietly and reassuringly to you now?*

3. *The poet Dante Gabriel Rossetti wrote:*

> *Deep in the sun-searched growths the dragon-fly*
> *Hangs like a blue thread loosened from the sky:-*
> *So this wing'd hour is dropt to us from above.*
> *Oh! clasp we to our hearts, for deathless dower,*
> *This close-companioned inarticulate hour*
> *When twofold silence was the song of love.*

What does this poetry mean to you in terms of silence, love, and faith?

4. *Abraham Joshua Heschel noted that*

> *The ineffable [God] will only enter a word in the way in which the hour to come will enter the path of time: when there shall be no other hours in the way. It will speak when of all words only one will be worthwhile. For the mystery is not always evasive. It confides itself at rare moments to those who are chosen. We cannot express God, yet God expresses His will to us. It is through His word that we know that God is not beyond good and evil. Our emotion would leave us in a state of bewilderment,* if not for the guidance we received. (Man Is Not Alone, 99-100)

Does this comment speak to you of the need sometime for undistracted quiet and openness in your life?

PRAYER

Adonai, You and I know the doubts and insecurities that have been part of my life. All of us, created in Your image, question whether we are truly living as You wished. And yet, even when I did not fully understand or accept it — in the midst of my turbulence and uncertainty, my pain and fatigue — You were there. You led me to the still waters of Your compassion and love, and You do so even at this moment. Help me, Lord, to drink deep from Your still, clear waters — and to share them with others. As You nourish my body, I pray that You will continue to nourish my soul. Walk along my sometimes uncertain path with me today so that I may be reassured of Your presence and surrounded by Your calm. Guide me and enable me to guide others to the tranquil waters that You have promised. Blessed are You, Adonai, who gives calm to the weary.

Psalm 23

65

He will restore my soul

There is a simple Hebrew prayer I recite every morning. It translates as follows:

> I am giving thanks to You, O King, who gives and sustains life; for You have returned my soul to me with compassion; great is your faithfulness."

This Hebrew prayer is the complement to the Christian prayer, "Now I lay me down to sleep, I pray the Lord my soul to keep. . . ."

The prayer from the Christian tradition asks the Lord to guard our soul while we sleep. In the Hebrew tradition, gratitude is expressed for the return or "restoring" of the soul. The Hebrew of the 23rd psalm can be translated as "restores" or "returns."

What a rich image this is — that God not only will replenish our energy when we are exhausted, but that we can in our rest entrust to Him our very souls, which He will faithfully guard and give back to us renewed and empowered for a new day. Or that in those times when we feel that we have lost our soul, our sense of our very meaning and purpose in life, the God who watches over His sheep can give this back to us. So great is his faithfulness.

FOR FURTHER REFLECTION

1. *Thomas Moore, author of the bestseller* Care of the Soul, *writes: "The great malady of the twentieth century . . . is loss of soul." Was there ever a time when you felt you had "lost your soul," that it had deserted you? Describe or reflect on that time. Do you sometimes feel today that you have lost your soul — your sense of your own meaning and worth? Do you deeply miss your career? Do you miss other responsibilities that gave significance to your life? Responsibility for your family, perhaps? Responsibilities in your community? In your synagogue or church?*

2. *Do you ever feel that you neglect your soul? "When the soul is neglected," says Thomas Moore, "it doesn't just go away . . . it appears in obsessions, addictions, violence, and loss of meaning." What do you think he means by that?*

3. *Do you pray to God to restore your soul in your life today? What are new ways to restore your soul that are still open to you at this time in your life — or ways that may not have been open at an earlier stage in your journey?*

4. *How can you help to restore someone else's soul? Perhaps your neighbor's or your roommate's? Perhaps the caregiver who herself is feeling stressed and depleted by life? Have you ever opened your soul up to another person? Are you willing to hear the pain in another's soul as well as his or her joy?*

5. *Have you ever wondered whether you could help to restore someone else's soul — and thereby your own soul — by forgiving that person for some mistake or wrongdoing?*

PRAYER

Adonai, sometimes, I have had to search for my soul. In anger or pain, frustration or loneliness, I felt I had lost my soul, or that it had deserted me. Now I know that it is never lost and that it sits before You at each moment, guarded by You both day and night. Now I know that I need not search in panic or ever doubt my soul's security. Your watchful gaze guards it, and when I open myself up to You, it is restored to me. Between the beats of my heart and the pauses in my breaths, there is my soul, which You restore to me each moment of my life. Blessed are You, Adonai, by whose word the world and my soul are recreated each day.

He will lead me along paths of righteousness for His own purposes

The Hebrew phrase *vemagelaa tsedeq* means much more than the usual translation — "paths of righteousness." In its most basic sense, the word *tsedeq* means "that which is ultimately right." Abraham Joshua Heschel remarked that

> Even though we may be unable to attain perfect righteousness, we at least cherish it as an ideal, as the finest of norms, and are even able to implement it to some degree. (*Man Is Not Alone*, 132)

And the meaning of *vemagelaa* is much more powerful than simply "paths." In its most basic sense it also implies "a purposeful course."

God, the psalmist tells us, leads us on a purposeful course which He has designed to direct us to what is ultimately right or righteous. One of the ways in which we, as Jews and Christians, discover what are the "paths of righteousness" is through prayer. In his popular work *On Becoming a Musical, Mystical Bear,* Matthew Fox writes:

> If prayer is, at its primary level, a response to life, it should be borne out of the prayer of the great prayers of history. Does such a description of prayer do justice to the prayer of the Jews and of Jesus and, if so, in what sense might their grasp of prayer alter or deepen the understanding of prayer we have arrived at as a response to life?
>
> The culture into which Jesus was born, whose language he spoke, and to which he was assimilated, was a powerful culture; that is, the Jewish people emphasized prayer in their recorded histories of the Old Testament. Not only the psalms, which are for

the most part poetic prayers, but the books of the prophets, the historical books, and, indeed, almost every book that makes up the history of the Jewish people reports praying by these same people. (51-52)

The psalmist then tells us why God leads us in the path of righteousness: "for the sake of His own name." In other words, when we choose to follow God in the path of righteousness, even when we may not fully understand it, we are honoring His name and honoring Him as the Creator. "What is it that the LORD requires of you," asks the prophet Micah, "but to do justly, love mercy and walk humbly with Your God" (6:8)? And, in Psalm 100 we are told: "Know that the LORD (Adonai), He is God; it is He that hath made us, and not we ourselves; we are His people, and the flock of His pasture" (3-4).

FOR FURTHER REFLECTION

1. *Reflect on a time when you thought that you wanted to pursue a particular path or direction, but something inside di-*

rected you in a way that was ultimately better for you. What was the occasion and how did you discover that your decision was ultimately right?

2. Is moving in the right direction sometimes more difficult for you now, perhaps because you have lost physical and emotional stamina?

3. We live in a time of constant change and ambiguity. Accepted values seem to change as we get older, and we are not always sure where the paths of righteousness lie. How has your concept of what is ultimately right or wrong changed as you have aged? What does mercy mean to you and how can you give it to others — neighbors, caregivers, family, fellow residents in your retirement or nursing home?

4. Do you pray to God not only about your own needs but also for guidance in discovering and following what are the paths of righteousness in your life today? Do you think about doing this for "His name's sake"?

5. Think of a contribution you made and continue to make to others that gives you a sense of doing justly and walking humbly with your God.

6. The writer of Proverbs said, "Righteousness delivers from death" (10:2). What do you think that comment means? Is

there a sense in which we live on in this world through our
acts of righteousness?

⌘

PRAYER

Adonai, I know that You have always wanted me to do well, not
only in the material aspects of my life, but more importantly in
my spiritual path. You want me to succeed and to know content-
ment. You want me to be an example for others. In many ways,
my life is a reflection of Yours. Throughout my life You have pro-
vided me with role models and a clear sense of right and wrong.
You have led me in the path of the righteous and merciful, even
when I was reluctant to follow. You have shown me the way and
You have guided me through the narrows of life. This day help me
to know that path on which You would have me travel with You.
Hold my hand gently in Yours, and walk with me. Blessed are
You, Adonai, who has taught me righteousness, mercy, and humil-
ity.

Even though I shall walk in the valley of death's
shadow, I shall fear no evil, for
You are with me

If a Christian or Jewish audience were asked to identify the most familiar line from this psalm aside from "The LORD is my shepherd," that line would be: "Even though I walk through the valley of the shadow of death. . . ." We have each experienced death and the loss of those we knew and loved; and we have survived it. We may have deep wounds and sometimes even lifelong scars, but we are not alone in our experience and, most importantly, God has not abandoned us.

Death is inescapable. We can constantly improve the quality of life and maybe even the length. But death — or the end of the consciously knowable life — is certain. Death's shadow is just behind our shoulder, even when its shadow cannot be seen. Here the psalmist is helping us to understand that we must all experience loss as a reality of human life. He is also reassuring us that while we will experience the death of others whom we love, God will be with us even in this time that feels like ultimate aloneness.

Secure in our knowledge of God's presence with us, we must embrace life with as much caring and compassion as we possibly can. Eleanor Roosevelt once said, "When you cease to make a contribution, you begin to die." Every one of us has a contribution to make. Smile. Question: "How are you?" "How's your grandson?" "Did you have a nice weekend?" "May I help you with your coat?" These are the contributions that enhance life — yours and others'.

The psalmist does not ask that we reject whatever apprehensions we may have about our death or the death of those whom we love; rather that we understand that through all of death and loss, "You are with me." For this reason the writer of 1 Corinthians can say with surety, "O death, where is thy sting? O grave, where is thy victory?" (15:55). Psalm 91, too, offers this reassurance: "Whoso dwelleth under the defense of the Most High shall abide under the shadow of the Almighty."

FOR FURTHER REFLECTION

1. There are many challenges in life that feel like the "valley of the shadow of death." Short of our bodily death, we may fear — or mourn — the death of our independence, of our youthful zest. Can you recall a challenge or responsibility that almost scared you to death? What fears today make you think of that valley? What got you through those fears?

2. What is your greatest fear regarding death? What is your most private hope?

3. The poet John Donne reassured us of death's inability to crush our spirit:

> Death, be not proud, though some have called thee
> Mighty and dreadful, for thou art not so;
> For those whom thou think'st thou dost overthrow
> Die not, poor Death. . . .

What do these words mean to you?

PRAYER

Adonai, often have I walked through the valley of death's shadow. Many are the times I have stood at the grave of a relative or friend. How many are the times I have felt lonely and deserted, angry, afraid, and surrounded by evil? Because I chose to love, I experienced loss and disappointment. Because I cared about others, I felt their pain and saw the evil of disease and despair consume them. And I am still here! I need not fear the evil that exists in the world because You are with me. I may not see You and those I love in the ways I wish, or hear Your voice or theirs when I want it most, but I do know that You are with me. There have been and there will be times when I must grieve. Help me to find the courage and strength I need within the soul You have daily returned to me. Blessed are You, Adonai, who has implanted within me eternal life.

Your spear and Your staff, they will give me comfort

A shepherd, even today, often carries two important implements with him: a rod, which is a type of club designed to frighten and beat off the enemies of his flock, and a staff, sometimes referred to as a shepherd's crook. The rod is to protect and the staff is to guide. With the crook in his staff, the shepherd can also pull a sheep to safety if it has slipped down a cliff or become entangled by its wool in brambles and thorns. And the One Shepherd, whom we know as God, carries both rod and staff and gives us the reassurance of both at all times.

A student once shared with me a story about a Basque shepherd. This shepherd came from a family in which the men had been shepherds for generations. They knew and understood the ways and needs of sheep. Each night as the Basque shepherd would gather in his flock of sheep, he would have each of them pass under his staff. In this way he could carefully check the ears and heads for burrs and cuts. At his side he would keep a jar of olive oil and one of water. After removing burrs or insects from the sheep's ears, he would wash them with water and then place the olive oil on the wound to help it heal. He also had fresh water for the sheep to drink at the end of the day. Again, the psalmist's image of the shepherd and the sheep encourages us to understand that God is infinitely caring of us, his flock.

In Hebrew, the word *shivtecha,* "your rod," can also mean "spear" or "lance." The psalmist here presents an image of God ready at any moment to defend us against whatever threatens us — while also gently shepherding us along with an occasional and gentle prod from his staff. Our sense of protection comes from knowing that there is One who wants both to protect and to guide us through life. The Hebrew word used for "they will give me comfort" is the same word used by the prophet Isaiah when he reassures the Hebrew people with the glorious phrase, "Be comforted, be comforted, My people . . ." (40:1).

In the biblical period, the kings were often considered the shepherds of the people of Israel. Too often, however, the kings were primarily concerned with their own wealth and ambitions and less with the welfare of their flocks. The prophet Ezekiel prophesies against the corrupt kings and says, "The Lord GOD (Adonai) says, Ah, you shepherds of Israel, who have been tending your-selves! Is it not the flock that the shepherds ought to tend? You partake of the fat, you clothe yourselves with the wool, and you slaughter the fatlings; but you do not tend the flock. You have not sustained the weak, healed the sick, or bandaged the injured; you have not brought back the strayed or looked for the lost" (Ezekiel 34:2-4). Similarly, the book of John (10:1-18) speaks of Jesus as the good shepherd who would lay down his life in defense of his sheep.

FOR FURTHER REFLECTION

1. *Have you experienced particular times when you felt mysteriously guided and protected? Are you able to look back at times when it seemed you must have been guided, though you did not realize it at the time? Do you still feel that protective hand?*

2. *Often God uses others to shepherd us. Our parents. Our teachers. Our friends. Our minister or rabbi. Who are your shepherds now?*

3. To whom can you now be a shepherd? The prophet Isaiah felt responsible to comfort the entire nation of Israel. If you could comfort one person or group, who would it be? What would you wish to do?

4. Are there times when you feel insensitively herded rather than shepherded? Do you ever feel lost and wonder who will find you?

5. Is there someone you would like to hit with your rod? Another you might want to rescue with your staff?

6. Do you feel you are being treated justly and that you receive the care and dignity due to one of God's sheep?

———⚬⚬⚬———

PRAYER

Adonai, today I seek Your protection from all that is beyond my control; and your guidance as I strive to live my life as fully as possible. Guard me from the depression and recriminations that pursue me, and comfort me with the staff of Your gentle leadership. Help me to be open to Your presence. Encourage and enable me to encourage others. Show me the gentle ways in which I might use my own "staff" to encourage others, and my "rod" to demand *justice and caring where there is too little. Enable me to bring comfort to myself and to others; the simple comfort of a touch or a reassuring smile. Blessed are You, Adonai, who gives strength to the weary.*

You will prepare a table for me in front of my enemies

In ancient times, as we saw earlier, kings were often thought of as shepherds, and here in these lines we have an image of a rich banquet set before us by a royal host.

That God "prepares a table" for us is acknowledged daily as we recite blessings and prayers before and after our meals. In the Hebrew blessing recited before meals, one phrase thanks God for bringing forth bread from the earth. The rabbis have long understood this as a reference to a messianic time, when it will be as though bread simply comes forth from the earth. In this image of that messianic era, all people will have their basic food, shelter, medical, and emotional needs met — as though bread came forth from the earth.

But here the psalmist takes us even further into our understanding of our relationship with God. He is reassuring us that *now,* as well as in the future, God will provide our daily sustenance for us. Again, we are assured that "we will not lack." Indeed, what we have set before us is not only adequate but abundant, if only we have eyes to see.

Another assurance is given here. The table, from which we will eat, be it real or symbolic, will be perfectly visible and obvious to those who have doubted, perhaps ridiculed, our beliefs. The Hebrew mind sees those who ridicule our beliefs less as physical enemies and more as narrow-minded, "self-bound" individuals who cannot see what the religious person sees. In Jewish tradition, they are entitled to their doubt, but they are not entitled to belittle or deride the belief of the other! For doing so is an offense not only to us but to God. Commenting on the persecution of the Jews in his *Reflections on the Psalms,* the Christian writer C. S. Lewis suggests that if we look at the anger of the Jewish people — here reflected in the phrase to "prepare a table in the presence of my enemies" — "we find they are usually angry not simply because these things have been done to them but because these things are manifestly wrong, are hateful to God as well as to the victim" (30). In front of these people, not for spite or derision, God will prepare my table and they will see the power of my faith and of my God.

The problems that confront us in the presence of our "enemies" as we age are often loneliness, loss of status and relationship, and diminished abilities. The psalmist is saying: "I may not walk as steadily as I once did. Sometimes I do not see or hear or understand as clearly; but I am here, and God — my shepherd — is here with me. You enemies who want to remind me about who and what I am not — you are not as powerful or as close to me as is my shepherd who invites me — unconditionally — to His table."

FOR FURTHER REFLECTION

1. *How, perhaps in spite of certain losses in your life, are your basic needs — physical, emotional, spiritual — being met? Who are your shepherds here?*

2. *Can you think of ways in which, beyond having your basic needs filled, you are blessed with an abundance of gifts? Can you recognize something special and good that happened to you today? The unexpected visit of a friend? Of a grandchild? The wonderful slant of the sun on the golden autumn trees beyond your window?*

3. *Can you remember just sitting around the kitchen table as a child and as an adult? What made it so special? Who made it memorable?*

4. *Who sits now with you at your table for dinner? What is most pleasant about him or her? Was there someone who challenged your faith in painful ways? What were the ways and what was the result? Were you able to view this not as a threat but as an opportunity to be a shepherd to someone else?*

5. *If you could invite someone to "your table," what value or belief would you want most to share with him or her? What*

menu would you fix? What memories would you share? What hopes? What fears?

PRAYER

Adonai, I know that You nourish my body and my soul daily. You have provided me with food for my body and encouragement for the challenges I must daily face. Today, I pray not only for myself and for all that You provide. I pray too, that You will help me to reach out to others who do not yet appreciate Your gifts and faithfulness. To those who doubt, let me be an example of certainty. To those who are self-absorbed, let me be a model of otherliness and caring. Help me to reach out to others and to "invite them to my table." Blessed are You, Adonai, who has implanted understanding and growth within each person.

You have anointed my head with oil

Oil was often used in biblical times as a healing balm. It might be placed on the head of a sheep to salve a wound or on the head of a guest to soothe the harsh effects of the desert sun. But in the Bible, to be anointed could also mean to be ordained by God. Anointing often referred to the way in which one was designated as special by God or by one of God's messengers. Prophets and kings were anointed with oil. And prophets and kings could in turn anoint others to special callings.

Anointing, then, conferred a special status on the individual. And it is very important here to note that the psalmist is saying that God, the shepherd-king, has anointed *my* head with oil. Each of us, then, is anointed. Psalm 28:9 reminds us that "The LORD is my strength; and He is the wholesome defense of His anointed."

For over thirty years I have placed my hands on the heads of infants and convalescing and dying people to anoint and bless them as they enter life or struggle against death. The experience has been very powerful for them and for me as well. And each time I realize that

I am a servant of the God who anoints them through me.

Father Henri Nouwen taught that each of us is the beloved of God, that each of us is truly anointed for specific purposes. Nouwen, like the psalmist, would constantly remind his readers that every person is the chosen, the beloved, the anointed one. We have been anointed with a royalty and dignity that is beyond mere kingship — even when we feel powerless. Anointing also brings with it special expectations. We who are commissioned in this way are expected to live a highly purposeful life, consistent with our particular calling or callings. We are also expected to live a highly intentional moral life.

FOR FURTHER REFLECTION

1. *Think about a time when you felt that God anointed you with a special blessing. Was it direct? Did someone you love confer it on you? Think about how it happened and how you felt.*

2. *Many people, as they grow older and retire from their careers*

or find themselves in a new situation in their lives, struggle to find their new callings in life. What might you be anointed to do at this stage of your journey? In your new situation, can you see and accept — even embrace — other important callings? To family? To grandchildren? To the care of others in your community? To volunteer tasks in your synagogue or church? Are you able to serve a few hours a month on some committee or board?

3. *Can simply being more attentive, rather than busy and active, be an important calling?* "Listen to your life," the author Frederick Buechner has said. "See it for the fathomless mystery that it is. In the boredom and pain of it no less than in the excitement and gladness: touch, taste, smell your way to the holy and hidden heart of it because in the last analysis all moments are key moments, and life itself is grace" (Listening to Your Life, 2).

4. *Jacob blessed and, in a way, anointed each of his children before his death. With what blessing would you anoint those you love? Many of us remember priceless advice from our grandparents. Can you now, perhaps with the wisdom that comes only with age, mentor those who are younger and help them to discern their particular callings?*

PRAYER

Adonai, You have anointed me with a love and constancy that are unconditional. Nowhere else in my life is love and acceptance so absolute. In my darkest hours and even in my darkest thoughts, You are with me. If I close my eyes and imagine a beautifully set table, I see all those whom I love around it. They are laughing and crying because we are all reunited. Each is eating his favorite food and each is taking delight in the other's joy. And we are all engaged in conversation about our lives and our beliefs and our closeness to one another and to You. We sit under a canopy of protection, so that the sun will not smite us by day, nor the moon at night. Blessed are You, Adonai, who fills my eyes with wonder and anoints my head with the oil of unconditional love.

My cup is satisfaction

The Hebrew word often translated as "overflows" can also refer to "satisfaction." The psalmist is telling us that while we envision ourselves sitting at the festive table with family and friends, we will know a deep satisfaction; we will be filled to overflowing. This passage can be understood as futuristic, referring to the table and cup which will be prepared for us in the afterlife. Or it can be seen to refer to how our needs are met today — even when we are not fully attentive or aware.

We all know people who look at life as though their cup is always half full. We also know people who always feel that their cup is half empty. I was once asked: "Rabbi, what is the difference between a cup that is half full and one that is half empty?" I replied: "The one who sees his cup as half full leaves room for God to fill the rest of his life. The one who sees the cup as half empty depends only upon himself and leaves no room for God." The psalmist is telling us that when we trust in God and choose to believe, our cup — the very vessel of our being — is not only filled, it is filled to overflowing! As we age, we learn that in certain ways we may need less to "fill our cup." Our appetites may lessen and the full meals and the things we used to look forward to — and believed we needed — no longer appeal to us. We find more satisfaction simply in life itself, even if it is a slower and in some ways more restricted life.

Even now, at age sixty, I am already more satisfied with a small meal and with less food. What fills me to deepest satisfaction are memories and an awareness of the feelings and dreams of my children and grandchildren, as they continue to grow and to experience the richness of life — as I now shepherd them with wisdom I did not have earlier. I have begun to understand the prophecy of Joel:

> And it shall come to pass afterward that I will
>   pour out my spirit
> Upon all flesh; and your sons and your daughters
>   shall prophesy,
> And your old men shall dream dreams,
>   your young men shall see visions. (2:28)

The dreams of age bring a past, a present, and a future with them, and are to be savored — moment by moment — and need not be feared.

FOR FURTHER REFLECTION

1. How did you picture the "overflowing cup" when you were younger? How do you think of it today? Do you ever feel that you are overflowing with something wonderful?

2. Who in your life was the optimist, whose cup was always at least half full? Who was the pessimist with the half-empty cup?

3. Do you worry that your cup might run dry? That you will become financially dependent? Or dependent in some other distressing way?

4. Do you sometimes feel that you have lost your appetite for anything at all?

5. Sometimes our lives are so filled with other things — with responsibilities, with sheer busyness, with anxiety, and sometimes with anger and bitterness — that we have no capacity left for joy. What prevents you today from making room for joy?

6. Picture your day as a beautiful chalice or kiddush cup to be filled as you would wish. How would you fill it? With whom would you like to share it?

7. *What gives you a sense of satisfaction today? How can you help another — family, friend, resident, or caregiver — also feel satisfaction?*

PRAYER

Adonai, my life has been so filled! Days were often occupied with family and friends; and the nights were filled with responsibilities and times of leisure.

Sometimes I wondered how I would do all that was required of me. Work and family and friends; such a full cup! Now there are times when my cup is filled with time and memories — and even some anger and regret. Today I ask that You help me to leave room in my cup for all that You would show me. Show me, too, opportunities to help another to fill her cup just a bit more with the joy You and I can bring. Help me, also, to look carefully at my regrets and to move beyond the emptiness they bring and forward to a cup overflowing with acceptance. Blessed are You, Adonai, who fills my life and cup.

Surely goodness and unconditional love will pursue me all the days of my life

The Hebrew word *chesed* is often translated in the Christian tradition as "grace" and in the Jewish tradition as "lovingkindness." In both traditions it implies an unconditional love. Here, almost at the very end of the psalm, the psalmist is rejoicing with us! No matter how far you stray, no matter how rotten you feel, I, the psalmist, am telling you that an unconditional love or acceptance is waiting for you — in fact, is pursuing you! Here is what the Christian writer Frederick Buechner has written about the unconditional goodness of grace:

> The grace of God means something like: Here is your life. You might never have been, but you *are* because the party wouldn't have been complete without you. Here is the world. Beautiful and terrible things will happen. Don't be afraid. I am with you. Nothing can ever separate us. It's for you I created the universe. I love you. (*Listening to Your Life,* 289)

One of the popular television shows in recent years

asks, "Who wants to be a millionaire?" The message for many is that if you were a millionaire, all your financial and personal needs and wants would be addressed. The psalmist is posing a much deeper question: "Would you like to be loved just because of who you are?" And each of us, assured that there are no conditions or hidden costs attached, would respond — YES! There are no gimmicks, no strings, no subscriptions to buy, just pure, one hundred percent *chesed*. Goodness and unconditional love are available to us — and all we have to do is open ourselves to them.

But there is more. It's not just that goodness and unconditional love are *available* to us if we seek them out. They *pursue* us! Instead of being pursued by our *enemies*, says the psalm, we are pursued by goodness and lovingkindness. The psalmist is telling us that just as loss and disappointment pursue us, so too do goodness and total acceptance. We try to run *from* loss and disappointment. We have not been taught how to run *to* grace and lovingkindness. Don't run from goodness, says the psalmist — grace and lovingkindness are running toward you, pursuing you, asking only that you slow down and accept them as the gifts of God. They are here for you every day of your life. Just allow them to embrace you!

FOR FURTHER REFLECTION

1. *Imagine that God has been pursuing you; knocking at the door of your heart. See yourself opening that door and greeting God. What would you expect to hear and what would you like to say?*

2. *Do you remember a period of "courtship" or "dating" when you pursued the one you love — or were pursued? How did that feel? Is there a relationship or feeling you would like to pursue and experience today?*

3. *In the book of Genesis we read that Sarah, late in life, laughed at the idea that she could still know joy. Do you feel there is still room in your life for joy and uncomplicated love? Would you like to have such an experience? What makes you resistant? What gets in the way? Anger? Frustration with your circumstance? Pride and your refusal to welcome help? Worrying about being a "bother"? How can you get beyond*

these things and open yourself to joy, sometimes in unexpected ways? C. S. Lewis titled his famous autobiography Surprised by Joy. Can you recall a time when you were "surprised by joy?"

4. Who needs to be pursued by you and shown goodness and love? Whom do you want to pursue you?

PRAYER

Adonai, sometimes it is difficult for me to believe that I can be loved, pursued as one who is desirable and worthy. And yet You, O God, choose to pursue me each moment of my life and to whisper, "I love you and I care about you." Now I see that those who care for me and provide for me are indeed your messengers, engaging in actions and activities of love and caring. Your love revives a joy and youthfulness too long forgotten. On this day of my life, help me to open my heart and soul wide to the gifts you are offering. Show me the myriad ways in which I may share them with others. Blessed are You, Adonai, who loves each person.

And I will dwell in the house of Adonai for days without end

Both the Jewish and Christian traditions believe in some form of afterlife. Moses Maimonides, a 12th-century rabbi and scholar, has written that there can be no way of comparing the good of the soul in the world to come with the physical goods of food and drink in this world. That good in the world to come is beyond all our understanding and incomparable beyond all our imagination. And in rabbinic literature there are frequent references to the afterlife as a time that is "all Sabbath" and a "heavenly academy" in which all the righteous are taught by God.

In this concluding line of the psalm, the psalmist is telling us that just as Adonai, the merciful God, is at the very beginning of life, so, too, God is there at the end. After this life, the psalmist reassures us, we will live in God's house in a manner that is beyond time and beyond our limited understanding. No clocks; no routines; no set schedules . . . just continuity beyond time. When we die we will not be forgotten, but remembered and embraced by eternity and God. Adonai will surround us as the womb surrounds the infant, and we will know safety and security — forever.

FOR FURTHER REFLECTION

1. *Imagine the most wonderful experience of your life and the people with whom you have shared it. What would it feel like to hold onto that experience and those persons forever? If you could pick the people with whom you would spend eternity, who would they be?*

2. *In your lifetime you have probably lived in many homes and places. Talk about the special memories you have of each of these houses. What would make your present dwelling place more acceptable to you?*

3. *If you could select two or three of your most cherished values — and know that they could be perpetuated forever — what would they be? What values should be granted to all people? What values should be demanded of all people?*

4. *Can you recall a day that you hoped would never end — one*

that you wanted to hold on to forever? Have you had days
that seemed to never end?

PRAYER

Adonai, God of mercy and love, I know now that You — moment
by moment — invite me to dwell within the world of worlds —
Your home. I accept Your promise to be with me for all time and
under all circumstances. I know too, that this body is the tempo-
rary body You have given me, but that You have also prepared a
shelter for me that is more splendid than any I could imagine. I
ask that on this day You help me to live fully within the limita-
tions of this body that You have given me — and that you help me
to accept Your invitation to dwell with You, now and always — in
security and love. Help me to convey this sense of security and
promise to others whom I love and respect, that they, too, may
dwell "in the house of Adonai for days without end." Blessed are
You, Adonai, who plants immortal life within each of us.

Sing to Adonai a Song That Is New

שירו ליהוה שיר חדש

———— ✼ ————

PSALM 98

Psalm 98

1 O sing unto the LORD a new song; for he hath done
    marvellous things: his right hand, and his holy arm,
    hath gotten him the victory.

2 The LORD hath made known his salvation: his
    righteousness hath he openly showed in the sight of
    the heathen.

3 He hath remembered his mercy and his truth toward
    the house of Israel: all the ends of the earth have
    seen the salvation of our God.

4 Make a joyful noise unto the LORD, all the earth:
    make a loud noise, and rejoice, and sing praise.

5 Sing unto the LORD with the harp; with the harp, and
    the voice of a psalm.

6 With trumpets and sound of cornet make a joyful
    noise before the LORD, the King.

7 Let the sea roar, and the fulness thereof; the world,
    and they that dwell therein.

8 Let the floods clap their hands: let the hills be joyful
    together

9 Before the LORD; for he cometh to judge the earth:
    with righteousness shall he judge the world, and the
    people with equity.

Psalm 98

Sing to Adonai a song that is new,
Because He has worked wonders.

His right hand has brought Him deliverance,
And His arm has set him apart in a holy way.

Adonai has made known His deliverance;
Before the eyes of the nations He has revealed
    His righteousness.

Remember His unconditional love
And His faithfulness to the House of Israel:

All the ends of the earth do see
The deliverance of our God.

Shout for joy to Adonai, all the earth.
Break forth! Cry aloud! And make music
(In praise of God)!

Make music to Adonai with the lyre;
With the lyre and with a melodious voice,

With trumpets and the sound of horns,
Sing joyfully to the (real) king, Adonai.

Let the sea and its fullness make a thunderous sound,
The dry lands and all who inhabit them.

Let even the small rivers and rivulets clap their hands.
The mountains shout for joy together

Before Adonai, for He comes to judge the earth:
He will judge the world with righteousness,
The people with directness.

Psalm 98

Psalm 98

INTRODUCTION

I have suggested that Psalm 121 is a psalm of movement and that Psalm 23 is a psalm of rest. Psalm 98 is a psalm of rejoicing and pure exultation, of joy and reassurance. It is often referred to as one of the "enthronement" or "kingship" psalms in which the God whom we know in the Jewish and Christian traditions as sovereign over all the world — and over all the gods of the ancient world — is recognized as the only true God. This psalm may have been written in response to the deliverance of the Jews from Babylonian captivity, just as they had earlier been delivered from captivity in Egypt. And so the psalmist calls out for a "new" song of celebration. Throughout this psalm the reader is encouraged to join in a song that recognizes God's greatness. "Ours is a God who intervenes in history and in the history of our own lives," the psalmist tells us. The writer of this psalm is one who has chosen to celebrate all that God (here referred to as *Adonai,* the most merciful aspect of God's selfhood) has revealed to him and, ultimately, to all of us!

The psalmist sees that all life and indeed all parts of nature are in awe of God and are invited to participate in this most wondrous of symphonies. "Sing," encourages the writer, for "Adonai has worked marvels." "Sing," because of Adonai's deliverances and righteousness! "Shout for joy to Adonai, all the Earth," because everyone and everything has benefited from His lovingkindness and His faithfulness to all the house of Israel!

As you read this psalm, you will again discover that all life, all experience, is infused with God. God is in the dry lands and in the sea, in the mountains and in the smallest of rivulets. But God dwells also in the chambers of our hearts and within the walls of our rooms, wherever we are. Truly, "the Earth is the LORD's and all that dwells (or exists) therein" (Psalm 24:1).

Read this psalm of celebration and discover the many ways in which you today may sing your own new song of rejoicing. Patiently find your own voice — your own instrument — and remember too, the songs of yesterday.

Know that God awaits and encourages you to sing and to rejoice in all that you are; in the brokenness as well as in the wholeness.

This is also a victory psalm commemorating God's victory over the other gods of the past and over all that diminishes our lives. It calls us to celebrate God's victories in our own lives, at each age and stage of our journey. Each step you take and each breath you inhale, each object you see and the birds you hear, these are victories for you and for God.

Psalm 98

Psalm 98

Sing to Adonai a song that is new,
Because He has worked wonders

One of the greatest challenges in life is to find our own authentic voice with which to express our feelings of joy and gratitude, loss and pain. So often we feel that someone else has discovered the secret to happiness but that it eludes us. Others seem to know a melody or enjoy a sense of security that is foreign to us, and we want it too. In childhood we are taught words and rhymes and simple songs. (My three-year-old grandson Max loves to have his mom call me so he can sing the "E-I-E-I-O" refrain from "Old MacDonald Had a Farm"!) Eventually, we develop a vocabulary and we find the words necessary to express our feelings and our thoughts. By the time we are adults, we have probably acquired the necessary words, but, regrettably, we have also been taught to censure some of the joy of life. We lose some of the exuberance of our youth. And yet, each day of our lives presents us with an opportunity to sing a new song, simply because we are alive, simply because we are one of God's marvels. The writer of Psalm 98 was probably very much aware of this normal human struggle. He is encouraging us to sing a new song with whatever words or syllables or melodies — or even mumbling — that we have, because God has worked miracles. Indeed, you and I, whatever our age and with all of our abilities and disabilities, are ourselves among the miracles of God.

To say that aging is a challenge is an understatement. But as we age, we can find our own voices and songs, and we must make them heard — within the deepest recesses of our own hearts, by others, and by God. These utterances, however simple or profound, are what the psalmist and God want us to express. God wants that new song to come forth from us. The writer Frederick Buechner suggests that "Eight-year-olds like eighty-year-olds have lots of things they'd love to do but can't because their bodies aren't up to it, so they learn to *play* instead. Eighty-year-olds," he goes on to say, might do well to take notice. They can play at being eighty-year-olds, for instance. Stiff knees and hearing aids, memory loss and poor eyesight, are no fun, but there are those who marvelously survive them by somehow managing to see them as, among other things and in spite of all, a little funny.

Another thing is that if part of being a child . . . is that you don't have to prove yourself yet, part of the pleasure . . . the second time around [in the older years] is that you don't have to prove yourself any longer. You can be who you are and say what you feel, and let the chips fall where they may.

. . . There is something bright and still about them at their best, like the sun before breakfast. Both the old and the young get scared about what lies ahead of them, and with good reason, but you can't help feeling that whatever inner goldenness they're in touch with will see them through to the end. (*Listening to Your Life,* 202-3)

Can you allow yourself to be playful at your age? Have you noticed that when children visit nursing homes or your apartment, they are fascinated with the wheelchairs and ramps and love to have wheelchair races? They enjoy playing with the electrically controlled, adjustable mattress, and they think it's "cool" that you have meals delivered to your room. Have you ever thought — at least just thought! — about racing your wheelchair down the hall? Have you ever played with all the different settings you can figure out with your bed? Have you ever imagined that you are a guest at a fine resort and that all of your meals are being brought to you? That you have people to serve you in all kinds of ways — a valet, a cook, a maid, a personal shopper? Have you ever played with an idea or a hope and had a lively conversation with others about "what if?" That's what Buechner and the psalmist are suggesting to us. Play with life and sing a new song each day and rejoice. We cannot reverse reality, but we can play with it and even make new songs and marvels.

My mother, who struggled with diabetes and heart disease, liked to show some of the nursing home residents how far she could walk with the new prosthesis on her leg. She would race down the halls! Earlier in life, she also delighted in showing her granddaughters how she could flick her false teeth out with her tongue. My daughters used to squeal with delight at the playfulness of their Bubbe (the Yiddish word for grandmother).

With these thoughts in mind, we can now look at the beauty of Psalm 98. It is an invitation to rejoice in all the wonders of life from the realm of nature to the very nature of who we are as children of God. To "sing to Adonai a song that is new" is to see the wholeness of the world and to rejoice in its beauty and in our own individuality.

Here, the verb "to sing" is stated both as a command and as an invitation. "Today is a day to sing!" Why? "Because I am alive and God is very present and because He has worked wonders!"

An old Jewish story relates that a young boy walked into the back of the synagogue on Yom Kippur, the holiest day of the Jewish year. While the congregation was singing the traditional melodies of the holiday, the boy began to sing the Hebrew alphabet over and over again. Finally, one of the older men, becoming very annoyed, approached him and told him that he must sing the correct songs and melodies. The boy responded that he did not know the words or the melodies. "But," he continued, "I thought that if I could recite the alphabet over and over, God would construct the words and add the melodies!" That boy combined play and reverence and prayer!

So often we are afraid that we don't have the perfect and best words with which to approach God, and that playfulness does not become us. Why? I have always found it interesting that musicians do not "work" an instrument, they "play" it. And some of the very finest musicians — think of the great cellist Pablo Casals, who performed into his 90s — have played their instruments with greater and greater joy and depth as they aged. We might even say that you and I are instruments of God, meant "to be played!"

The psalmist is telling us we don't have to have words or melodies like those of poets and famous composers — or even those found in the prayer books. All we need, as the psalmist says elsewhere, are the "words of my mouth and the meditations of my heart." Sing, whistle, hum, put on a radio, record, or tape that has the music you would like to share with God and with yourself — and rejoice in this new day!

FOR FURTHER REFLECTION

1. *What new feeling or thought are you experiencing right now? Can you turn it into a song title? What would that title be?*

2. *Can you recall the first song you ever learned? Who taught it to you? Do you know the words and melody today? Will you sing it? What language is it?*

3. *What is your favorite song today? Who is your favorite singer?*

4. *Are there songs, or other pieces of music, that move you now more than they did when you were younger? Do you perhaps now understand and appreciate the words of such songs better than you once did? Perhaps the words of a favorite hymn? Why and in what way?*

5. *For some people the happiest song "Happy Birthday." For others it is a song learned in the church or synagogue. Every day is a birthday, and every day is a new world. Hum or sing "Happy Birthday," or another song, to yourself or to a friend. Can you sing a song about your room? Even if it feels a little silly? About your food? Make up a four-line song about food or walking or sitting in the sunlight.*

6. *The psalmist tells us that God has done wonders and marvels in both nature and history. Share an event or experience of wonder that occurred in your life? Who was there to experience it with you and what made it so special? Study the flower in your room and see its wonder.*

7. *What is the best part of your day now? Who makes you want to sing? The man who takes care of your lawn and flowers or shovels your walk? Your roommate? The hairdresser? The custodian, recreation director, food server? Someone in your family? Who? Is there more than one?*

8. *What simple yet marvelous thing could you do today for someone else? A phone call, smile, card, compliment? What could you do for yourself?*

9. *What victory did you achieve as a child? What small victory now would make your day special? What small victory would make someone else's day special?*

———❧———

PRAYER

O God, it is so easy for me to miss the beauty that surrounds me. It is possible to miss the smallest gesture of kindness or the sound of a

solitary bird singing outside my window. Then I see instances of
beauty and care. Sometimes I feel that my words are inadequate.
How shall I sing a new song to You — to You who have heard every
song? How shall I sing to You from this foreign land called aging?
Help me to know that You will rejoice in my song regardless of
whether it has words; that You can hear the gratitude of my heart
and the still silence of my soul. You have worked wonders in nature
and in history and in the vessels of my own being. Let my life, how-
ever humble, be its own song to You; and let me listen leisurely to
the melodies and marvels that come moment by moment from You.
Blessed are You, Adonai, who brings a new song to my lips and ears.

His right hand has brought Him deliverance,
And His arm has set Him apart in a holy way

The Hebrew of this line is fascinating! Literally it reads: "His right [hand is implied] has brought Him deliverance, and [the] arm, His holy nature."

The English translation reads "set Him apart," but the verb in Hebrew really means, "to set apart in a holy way." The verb is *kadesh,* and it is used in almost every Hebrew blessing. This line tells us that God is set apart in his supreme holiness. But Father Daniel Helminiak (*Spiritual Development: An Interdisciplinary Study,* 146) reminds us that, according to the Hebrew Bible, "one is holy because one is related to God, one is like God. God is set apart in His holiness, and in our relationship to Him, we are also — each in our distinctive way — set apart and made holy. That is to say, the holy one is the one who does God's will, who is faithful to what God desires, who 'walks humbly with God'" (146).

In ancient Israel it was believed that the deliverance needed in this psalm was from foreign gods or from the enslavement of Egypt. Today, we want the assurance that God will reach out to us at every moment and protect us from the problems that beset us. We want and need to know that the right arm of God will support us. But we also need and must call out to a God who helps us discover daily our own power through our own holy relationship to him.

FOR FURTHER REFLECTION

1. *Do you ever marvel at the sheer power and glory and holiness of God? The Christian writer J. B. Phillips wrote a book called* Your God is Too Small. *Is your God too small? What in your life now can prevent you from seeing and exulting in His grandeur and holiness?*

2. *In the biblical period people believed that God had to prove His might. What are some of the ways in which you have seen God express His power in your life? How do you use God's power for others?*

3. *In what ways do you want to see that power made clearer in your life today? What loss do you want God to understand? What power do you want to see or feel?*

4. *Reflect on what it might mean that in your relationship to God you are also set apart and made holy. How would you like your own "right arm" to be strengthened? What is your own "right arm"? Each of us is unique, both in the eyes of God and in the hearts of others in our lives. And each of us has talents, ranging from cooking and gardening to listening and singing and drawing upon memories. What is one of your unique talents?*

5. *Do you have difficulty accepting yourself as set apart by God? Can you remember a time, maybe in elementary school, when you wanted to be like someone else? What did that feel like and how did you grow beyond it? When did you become the "real" you?*

6. *Whom do you admire today? What is admirable about you? What qualities make a person admirable? What qualities and experiences have set you apart?*

Psalm 98

⸺ ⧉ ⸺

121

PRAYER

O God, You have created me to be distinct and you have chosen me for holy purposes. Sometimes I can see and take joy in these purposes, and at other times I am blinded to them or they burden me. Help me to see and accept my uniqueness and all the joy that is involved in being set apart for a special relationship with You. So often I want to be like everyone else — or like one or two people who seem to have fewer demands on their lives. Sometimes I may keep people at arm's length, only because I am afraid. Enable and encourage me to see that in your eyes I am set apart for a special (kadesh) relationship with you; and that I can have an intimate

and holy relationship with others also. Help me to know that in
my brokenness and age, You accept me; that even in the distinc-
tiveness of my imperfection and limitations, You can draw me
closer to Your right hand of acceptance. Blessed are You, Adonai,
who has made me holy and distinct.

Adonai has made known His deliverance;
Before the eyes of the nations He has revealed
His righteousness

With these two lines an entire theological conversation
could be sparked — one that could last for hours! The
psalmist is telling us that Adonai has made known His
saving power before the eyes of *all* the nations of the
world. While only some have come to understand and ac-
cept that saving power, He revealed His righteousness in
ways that all could understand if they chose to do so.
What God has given to Israel is to be shared with all the
world (Davidson, 323).

The psalmist also introduces us to the Hebrew concept of *tsedaqah* or "justice." In Hebrew there is no word for charity; in its place is the concept of justice or righteousness. We do good deeds and live a moral life and care for one another because these are the ways in which we express and reveal God's own righteousness. In the book of Deuteronomy we read, "Justice, justice, you shall pursue" (16:20). Our life journey can be framed in justice because God has achieved a victory over all that is unjust. Pain and suffering, disappointment and distress, diminishment and daily defeat can be overcome if we accept God's victorious deliverance. "Down, but not out!" is a phrase used in boxing. Often we feel down and afraid, and God is telling us, "I will not count you out!"

C. S. Lewis once commented that many people think of Christianity as being all about morality, rules, duty, and guilt. "Yet it leads you on, out of all that, into something beyond. . . . Everyone there is filled with what we should call goodness as a mirror is filled with light" (*Mere Christianity*, 130).

And Jewish tradition notes that "Chief among the duties of the heart is the attuning of the soul into such perfect harmony with God that all right conduct and right thought must follow without effort on your part, because our will is one with His, through love" (*Gates of Prayer* 15:5).

Long ago, the rabbis began a practice known as "midrash," providing commentaries and further insights into biblical and later texts. One such midrash has Abraham speaking to God and saying, "If you want the world to exist you cannot insist upon complete justice; if it is complete justice you want, the world cannot endure" (Genesis Rabbah 49:20). We are all imperfect people living in an imperfect world. Our daily challenge is to pursue justice and to deliver others, if only for a few moments, from loneliness and despair — and to allow others, and God, to deliver us! Some of us are more able to take the care others offer us. And some are better at giving care. But we need both.

The book of Proverbs tells us that "Gray hairs are a glorious crown which is won by a righteous life" (16:31). And, "better a little with righteousness than great revenues with injustice" (16:8).

FOR FURTHER REFLECTION

1. *Do you think about yourself as "set apart" in your own special way, to be a mirror of God's righteousness? Think about C. S. Lewis's image of a mirror. To be a mirror, you need to make yourself available to the source you are to reflect. How do you open yourself, in your particular circumstances, to the righteousness of God? To be a mirror you also need to be a properly reflective surface. What are the ways in which you might blur or distort God's righteousness?*

2. *So many people sing songs of sorrow. What can you do today to help another to sing a new song of hope and deliverance? Do you see injustices around you that you might help to correct? Do you feel you are justly and righteously treated? Do you think you can speak out for the just and right treatment of your caregivers and neighbors?*

3. *What would be a righteous deliverance for you, today? What would help you to feel a sense of personal justice today? Do you sometimes feel that you should be delivered from the place where you now live? Or do you really need to be delivered from unrealistic expectations about yourself and from an*

inability to see the ways in which you can reflect God's righteousness in a new way?

4. William Shakespeare wrote:

> "A man may see how this world goes with no eyes. Look with thine ears: see how yond justice rails upon yond simple thief. Hark, in thine ear. Change places and, handy-dandy, which is the justice, which is the thief?"
> (King Lear IV:6)

Do these lines make you a little more sympathetic with another person?

Psalm 98

❦

PRAYER

O God, You have given me the power to do justly, to love mercy, and to walk with humility along my path. As I prepare for today's richness of experience and opportunity, help me to reach out to others in ways that reflect Your righteousness and deliverance. You delivered Israel from slavery and others from their personal bondage. Help me this day to act in just and merciful ways with those around me and to accept Your invitation to be delivered and

*to deliver another from moments of despair. With a smile or a
phone call or a brief note, I too can give* tsedaqah *to my world.
Blessed are You, Adonai, who invites me to enjoy and to share
righteousness and justice.*

Remember His unconditional love
And His faithfulness to the House of Israel

Again, we encounter the Hebrew concept of "lovingkind-
ness," *chesed,* which is often translated as "grace" in the
Christian community. It is also understood in both com-
munities as a form of unconditional love.

I once began to write an essay about unconditional
love. The longer I wrote, the more I began to realize that
there was no person in my life I truly loved uncondition-
ally. I had thought that I could turn to my wife or children
and say, "I just want you to know that no matter what you
do, I will always love you." The more I reflected on this

idea, the more I realized I could not make such a statement. All my human relationships are conditional and have expectations and even time parameters. This realization saddened me, but also gave me a deepened sense of the difference between the human and the divine. I shared my thinking with two close friends, one a Catholic nun and the other a Protestant from the Calvinist tradition. I asked: "Can you think of any relationship in which there is truly unconditional love . . . one in which you love or are loved simply because you are?" And each replied: "Only with God!"

Rabbi Wayne Dosick has written, "*Chesed* is God saying, 'It does not matter what you do, how you behave, how many mistakes you make, I am your God. And you are my child. I love you always and forever, with a deep, abiding, unqualified, absolute love'" (Dosick, 18-19). This is the love we all want on our journey.

The Hebrew word used here in Psalm 98 for "faithfulness" is *emunah,* which sounds like our word "amen." In fact, "amen" is derived from *emunah* and in Judaism is traditionally understood as "let it be," or "surely it is so."

It is customary in Judaism to recite a specific prayer

upon rising in the morning. In translation the prayer reads as follows: "I am expressing gratitude to You, O King, who gives and sustains life; for you have returned my soul to me, great is your faithfulness."

The psalmist continues and reminds us that God's lovingkindness and faithfulness have been demonstrated time and again through His relationship as He journeyed with the house, or people, of Israel. Throughout history (the contemporary psalmist would say) God's assurances and the fulfillment of His word have been given to the house of Israel — which would be understood as the Jewish and Christian communities. This, too, is worthy of a new song!

FOR FURTHER REFLECTION

1. *Can you recall times in your life when you received what seemed a gift of pure grace? In an unexpected gesture from a friend? In a sudden and radiant sense of God's beauty and goodness?*

2. *Do you sometimes find it hard to accept a gift because you haven't "earned" it? Because it offends your sense of self-reliance? Are you able to accept yourself even in your weakness and failures, because God accepts you? Has it ever struck you that pride, your sense that you can and must earn your own worth, is the cruelest and most demanding of taskmasters? That you need to be liberated from yourself?*

3. *Who have provided some of the most wonderful examples in your life of faithfulness and loving-kindness? To whom can you now show such faithfulness and loving-kindness? In what ways?*

4. *Do you feel God is always there with you and for you? Are there times when you feel abandoned by God — as if some conditional parameter had been set?*

5. *Timelessness is also called "eternity." How do you imagine eternity? Is there a psalm or other piece of religious literature that reminds you of God's eternal love? Do you feel part of eternity? Whom do you want with you through eternity?*

PRAYER

O God, to know that you love me even when I may not love myself — or feel worthy of love — offers me a sense of calm and reassurance. Through your unconditional lovingkindness and faithfulness, You see beyond my frailties and foibles, my faults and limitations. You see something within me that is eternal and you guard it out of the purest love. When I lie down You hold my soul ever so gently in your hands, and when I awaken You restore it to me, just as You restore my capacity to greet the new day. Accept, I pray, my gratitude for that which is restored to me; and help me to accept that which is no longer. Blessed are You, Adonai, who lovingly and faithfully holds me close and celebrates me!

All the ends of the earth do see
The deliverance of our God

The psalmist is overflowing with life and enthusiasm and wants us to hear his song: "See with your eyes! Hear with your heart and soul! Feel with all that God has given you! See the deliverance that is ours! Let every man, woman, and child, every baby and every older person rejoice — through all the nations and peoples of the world!" This is the exaltation and assurance the psalmist wants to share with us.

My late friend, Father Henri Nouwen, was the gifted author of over forty books and numerous articles. He was a spiritual guide for thousands of people because he was filled with an enthusiasm and a certainty about his beliefs and a commitment to share God's love and caring. Every occasion in life was an opportunity for Henri to share God's joy and his joy in God. To this same end the psalmist is saying: "Can you not see, have you not heard? God and all the goodness of God is surrounding us, and we only have to open our minds and hearts to enjoy it." Our eyes may be dim, perhaps by reason of our age, but the Light can shine in! "If I say," cries the psalmist in Psalm 139,

> "Surely the darkness will cover me,
>   and the light around me become night,"

even the darkness is not dark to you;
the night is as bright as the day,
for darkness is as light to you.

FOR FURTHER REFLECTION

1. *What images help you imagine the "ends of the earth"? What gives you the grandest sense of God's creation? A limitless seascape? A magnificent view of the Earth from a satellite?*

2. *Where do you most easily see God's goodness and wonders in your life? Is it in nature, in friends and family? When in your day are you most open to God? What makes that happen? What closes you off?*

3. *Age may dim the eye, but age can also bring wisdom, perspective, and illumination. Do you see and appreciate some things now much better than you did when you were younger?*

4. *When have you felt the absence of goodness? Was there a time in your life when you felt delivered by God? What was the occasion and were there other people involved with you? Do you remember who they were?*

5. *What does deliverance mean to you today? From what or whom do you want to be delivered today? Is there a darkness covering you that you desperately wish God to make as bright as day? To whom might you be able to offer deliverance and from what?*

PRAYER

O God, sometimes I cannot see or hear the goodness that surrounds me. Sometimes I feel so alone and isolated from all that fills life with meaning and beauty. Grant me the comfort to truly believe that You do know my step and that You do look upon all my ways. Reassure me that I cannot go from Your spirit or flee from Your presence. Deliver me from the doubts and depression that crouch at my doorstep. Just as You would show all the nations of the world Your power to deliver, show me the deliverance that heals my wounded heart and restores hope in my soul. Blessed are you, Adonai, who brings healing to those in pain.

Shout for joy to Adonai, all the earth.
Break forth! Cry aloud! And make music
(In praise of God)!

Can you imagine being so filled with joy, so ecstatic, that you want to just run and jump and sing and clash cymbals and shout? Could you imagine how wonderful it would be if all the people of the earth felt this way?

At the wedding of each of my daughters I wanted to express my happiness and delight to God in as many ways as I could. I wanted to sing, to make loud music, to share my exultation with as many people as possible. My wife and I had waited at least thirty years for each of these weddings, and our daughters had chosen their mates deliberately and well. I had the honor of officiating at each of these weddings, and I felt that no matter what I said, my words would never fully express my happiness.

When each of our grandchildren was born, we again cried loud and deep tears and rejoiced openly.

Wanting to share our joy with others and with God, my wife and I made contributions to our synagogue to purchase a baby changing station and a velvet cover for the main pulpit. We wanted to share our gratitude and blessings with our extended community.

In these exuberant lines, the psalmist is encouraging all the people — through all the ends of the Earth — to *see* and *exult* over the deliverance of our God. The psalmist wants us to know that this deliverance is not just a one-time event, but an ongoing and everlasting reality. It is available to all people who would choose to believe. It calls for music to be sung by heart and soul. Imagine the excitement of the psalmist as he writes this line and those to follow. He is imbued with God, intoxicated with certainty! "You are alive and God is alive and the world is beautiful even when you can't fully comprehend or see it. Sing, play, rejoice, express gratitude; live fully and intentionally today!"

In my own most joyous moments, even in fullness of health, I was of course limited by the ways in which I could outwardly express my gratitude to God. I could not afford a symphony, but I could sing! We could not make sure that every baby would be as loved and doted upon as would be our grandchildren, but we could make sure that every infant who came into Temple Emanuel would have a clean and safe changing station!

For each of us there is a way and a time to shout and rejoice — just as there is a way and a time to cry and to mourn. Even as we face death, says the psalmist in Psalm 16,

> I am ever mindful of the LORD's presence;
> He is at my right hand; I shall never be shaken.
> So my heart rejoices,
> My whole being exults,
> And my body rests secure.
> For you will not abandon me to Sheol
> Or let your faithful one see the pit.
> You will teach me the path of life.
> In Your presence is perfect joy;
> Delights are ever in Your right hand.

Psalm 98

———

137

As we progress on our journey through aging, there are times when we want to shout not out of joy but out of anger. Sometimes each of us is frustrated or disappointed. This shout is important, too. It does not distance us from God. When it is over, we may feel better and may be more open to the God who cares and hears and understands. Indeed, then we may be ready to sing, too.

FOR FURTHER REFLECTION

1. *Recall a time, in the past or recently, when you literally shouted for joy, when you couldn't contain yourself. What was the occasion? Was it a birth, marriage, graduation, new job, new friends? Were you alone or with another person? What simple thing would cause you to sing for joy today?*

2. *Psalm 98 is one of the most ecstatic of the psalms. Here is a quotation from Henri Nouwen that you may wish to ponder:*

> *"Ecstasy" comes from the Greek "ekstasis," which in turn is derived from "ek," meaning out, and "stasis," a state of standstill. To be ecstatic literally means to be outside of a static place. Thus, those who live ecstatic lives are always moving away from rigidly fixed situations and exploring new, unmapped dimensions of reality. Here we see the essence of joy. Joy is always new. Whereas there can be old pain, old grief, and old sorrow, there can be no old joy. Old joy is not joy! Joy is always connected with movement, renewal, rebirth, change —* in short, with life. (Lifesigns, 88)

3. *Did you ever take music lessons? Were they successful? Who wanted you to have the lessons? Did you enjoy them?*

4. *As you look back, did the music give another dimension to your life? Would you like music to play a larger part in your life today? What music would you like to hear right now? Are you able to listen to the radio?*

5. *If you could sing a new song or even an old one, even if your voice is less than perfect, would you want to sing it alone? With others? If with others, whom? In a choir or glee club? Can you sing with your caregiver? Does he or she have a favorite song?*

6. *If you could write your own song to God, what would the lyrics be? How loud can you sing?*

7. *What are other ways in which you can express your joy? You cannot hire an orchestra, but what thing* can *you do?*

8. *Can you recall a time when your joy in God was in the end greater because of a sorrow you endured?*

———∞———

PRAYER

O God, I do have a song to sing, to You and to all those who have helped me to become the person I am. I would sing to my parents and teachers and to each one who helped me along my way. Just as there are days when I want to shout: "Enough disappointment and enough limitations," so too there are days when I would sing and make the sweetest music to express my happiness about another day of life; about another opportunity to touch the lives of others and to have them reach out in such caring ways to me. Let a new song pour forth from my heart and soul, and help me to share my song and its blessings with others. As my soul is ever in your presence, so too may my song ever be upon Your heart. Blessed are you, Adonai, who gives voice to my many songs.

Make music to Adonai with the lyre;
With the lyre and with a melodious voice

When I finished my doctorate in 1978, my wife bought me a beautiful cello and made arrangements with a fine cellist from a local string quartet to give me lessons. I have always loved cello music, and certain compositions and musicians reach the deepest recesses of my being. I practiced my cello for about six months, and then realized that if I were really going to make music I also had to make a commitment to practice — regularly. Vocal and instrumental music, as well as prayer — the music of the soul — requires discipline and practice.

In time I realized that I was not ready to give my cello the time needed in order for it to truly make music. But I continue to delight in the instrumental music of others, and I regularly loan my cello to aspiring students. In the meantime, I have found my singing voice and I truly do delight in serving as the cantor during worship services. I sing to my grandchildren and love to sing duets with my wife. "And when you let forth the beautiful music that is within you," says the psalmist, "do it with the lyre and with your God-given voice!"

The lyre and the melodious voice suggest sounds of sweetness and intimacy. From this point onward the psalmist will encourage us to bring every one of our talents before God. For some it will be the voice and for others it will be a musical instrument. But what he wants us all to know is that in God's eyes we all have talents to share — writing, cooking, caring, listening, guiding, reaching out, sharing intimate stories of the past. All are talents to be shared with others and with the God who gave them to us.

Each of us is an instrument with a particular pitch and tone. We may bring our own solitary song before the Lord in the quiet of our room. Or we may blend our music wonderfully with the tones of others in a kind of chamber music of praise.

FOR FURTHER REFLECTION

1. *If you could write a song of praise to God, what would you most want to praise Him for?*

2. *If you could write a song about your life, what three words would you want to make sure were in it? Think of three words that would describe who you are and how you have lived.*

3. *What instruments would you want played to accompany your song? What instrument do you think best fits your character and personality?*

4. *Who are your favorite musicians — vocal or instrumental?*

5. *What is your favorite type of music and are you giving yourself the opportunity to listen to it? Do you remember when you used to say that you would listen more to music (or read or look at art) when you "had the time"?*

6. *Do you ever think of each of your talents as offering the possibility of song? What would it mean for your very life to sing? Do you ever imagine your life as an unfinished symphony? What part is still to come?*

7. *Members of string quartets and other chamber groups often speak of the importance of listening closely and intimately to the other instruments in the group, each with its distinctive tone, each with its distinctive line to play as part of the musical whole. Are you able to appreciate the contributions of others? Can you take genuine joy in the gifts brought by others, sounds that you yourself may not be able to make?*

———∞∞∞———

PRAYER

O God, there is so much to sing about in this life! I can sing about the finely tuned body and soul You have given me; about the won-

*ders of nature that surround me, in every season of the year; about
the experiences I have shared with family and friends. As I look
over the span of my years, I do see that there were moments when
I wanted to burst forth in song; to share my joy and excitement
with everyone around me. There were times of sadness, too, when
I wished someone would play a soothing melody on the harp or
lyre or sing to calm my pain and to bring rest to my wearied heart.
Help me this day to remember those sweet moments and to place
the sadness into a new perspective. Hold me close in Your accept-
ing hands, and let me know again that I am loved. Blessed are
You, Adonai, who listens to my many voices. Help me in turn to
listen with joy to the voices of others.*

**With trumpets and the sound of horns,
Sing joyfully to the (real) king, Adonai**

If the lyre and the melodious voice suggest sweet and inti-
mate sounds, trumpets and horns are grand and regal. In

ancient Israel it was customary to announce special occasions, especially the coronation of kings and the beginnings of new months, with a variety of horns. It was also usual to announce wars and battles and significant holidays in the same way. Even today, it is traditional to usher in the Jewish New Year with the sound of the ram's horn, known as the shofar.

Rabbi Moses ben Maimon (1135-1204), also known as Maimonides, reminds us of the summoning quality of the shofar and its sounds. He wrote:

Psalm 98

———

145

> It says: "Awake, ye sleepers, and ponder your deeds. Remember your Creator, and return to Him in penitence. Be not among those who miss reality in their pursuit of shadows, and waste their years in a quest for vain things. Look to your souls. Examine your acts. Forsake evil, all of its ways and thoughts, so that God may have mercy on you." (Rosten, 470)

Again, the psalmist is inviting us to use these traditional instruments to celebrate life and our relationship with Adonai, the King of all kings. "You are the cornet of God," he tells us, "Make your unique sound for all to hear." But the psalmist also knows that each of us has even more to bring to the coronation — our selves. It is as if the psalmist says to us today: "I know that in the past people made wonderful sounds with all manner of instruments; but the greatest instrument in the world is *you.* You may walk slowly and hear with difficulty. You may not see as well as you once did, but you can make a sound that brings joy to another and to yourself — and to God. You can do it with horns and other crafted instruments, and you can make it with your own God-given talents. It may be your own solitary sound, and it may be your sound as part of a full band or orchestra. I want, says the Lord, to hear it if it is solitary, and I want to hear it if it is in concert with other sounds. I want to hear it, because it comes from you. I have heard the brass and wind quartets, but the breath of your voice and thought is sweeter than all of them!"

FOR FURTHER REFLECTION

1. *Are there times when you sing for the pure joy of singing? What is the most joyous and celebrative event you can recall in your life? Do you have favorite celebrative music?*

2. *What do you praise God for most at this time in your life? When you reflect on the past? When you reflect on the present?*

3. *Are you truly open to joy? Or do you block it in some ways? What gets in the way? What can you do about this? Do you often feel refreshed after you exercise? What "spiritual disciplines" can you practice to make way for joy? Praying at regular times? Reading the Bible daily? Perhaps going through the discipline of memorizing Scripture? Have you thought about memorizing parts — or all! — of the psalms in the book you are now holding? The author Richard Foster wrote a bestselling book called* Celebration of Discipline: The Path to Spiritual Growth. *Reflect on the meaning of this title. Can you see how discipline can actually lead to joy?*

4. *Do you see yourself as an instrument to bring joy to others? Have you ever found joy yourself in giving joy to others?*

5. *Often in the psalms the call to praise God's wondrous deeds is*

linked to the call to seek justice and righteousness. Where in your life today do you feel especially called to pursue justice, especially for others?

Psalm 98

PRAYER

O God, who has given me a voice with which to make my joys and my wants known, and ears with which to hear the beauty of horns and the harshness of war's trumpets, let me add my voice to those who would seek peace in the world and within themselves. Help me to take the sounds of discord that are within me and around me and turn them into sweet sounds that others will hear and enjoy. Let my words be statements that convey the softness of the French horn and my call for justice be like the boom of the symphony's tuba. Let each word and every note filter through my heart and soul before it is uttered; so that it may reflect the sound that You would have me share with my world. Blessed are you, Adonai, who encourages me to express the music of the horns and the melodies that fill my heart.

Let the sea and its fullness make a thunderous sound,
The dry lands and all who inhabit them

Remember how the psalmist opened his own song to God
with the line, "Sing a new song unto Adonai"? Here, like
an inspired conductor with a listless orchestra, he is try-
ing to encourage as many of the musicians (you, me, the
sea, the heavens) as possible to see God's wonders in a
fresh way. Or perhaps, as we noted earlier, to celebrate the
deliverance of the Jews from a second captivity, their exile
in Babylon. "How shall we sing of God in a strange land?"
the Hebrews had cried in their exile. You and I may ask:
How can I sing of God in the strange confines of my
room, my illness, my diminished body — which can al-
most seem "foreign" to you when you look in the mirror
and remember what you once were.

"By the waters of Babylon," cried the Hebrews, "we sat
down and wept, when we remembered thee, O Zion. As
for our harps, we hanged them up on the trees that are
therein. For they that led us away captive required of us
then a song, and melody, in our heaviness: Sing us one of
the songs of Zion!"

For the Jewish people, Babylon was a "dry land" — a place without joy or song. They felt desolate and depressed. Their hope came from God through the prophets and through their collective memories. As we age, we journey through refreshing seas and barren dry places. We go through the valley of the shadow of death. And we drink from refreshing wells and streams. On that journey, we have many questions and doubts.

The Hebrews' answer was often to live as fully and as intentionally as possible through God's law and love, and to take every opportunity to celebrate and to rejoice and to hold onto all the joy they had experienced. At other times, like each of us, Israel just wept. Sometimes weeping is what we most need for the moment. Tears may clear our vision.

The psalmist is providing us with still another and reassuring vision. Usually we see the thunder of the sea as threatening, and we are afraid of it. In fact, the reference to the thundering sea may have been meant to remind the Hebrews of God's ancient enemies. Once they roared in defiance of God, but now even they pay homage to Him. The thunderous sound is part of a majestic symphony of praise. The psalmist then says, "No, not just the seas! I want the whole world to rejoice; not only the waters, but also the dry areas — everything and everyone!"

FOR FURTHER REFLECTION

1. *An old song says: "Sound the loud timbrel, o'er Egypt's dark sea!/The Lord hath triumph'd — his people are free." What sound or sight would represent freedom for you today? What type of freedom do you need and want? Do you want to share it with anyone else? Do you fear economic enslavement?*

2. *Recall a time when you stood before the thunderous roar of the sea, when it seemed like the whole world would come apart. What did that feel like? Did it frighten you? Does it frighten you today? Was someone with you?*

3. *Have you also stood before the thunderous roar of the sea and been exhilarated by the sheer beauty and power of the sound? Has it made you want to sound your own trumpet of praise?*

4. *Have you had the experience in life that what was most fear-*

some became instead an occasion to see God's goodness and glory?

5. Do you ever feel that you have the roar of thunder within you? What prompts it? What calms it? Do you sometimes feel that your life has become barren, like a desert? What kinds of things nourish and replenish you?

6. What is the most calming aspect of nature for you and what is the most disturbing? What is the most calming part of your own nature and what is most disturbing? What is most calming about your life now? What is most disturbing? Who makes you calm? Who disturbs you?

———∞∞∞———

PRAYER

O God, help me to see all of nature as Your gift. Let me experience my unique role in the unfolding of this wonderful symphony You have prepared. Let my singing and humming and even my silent remembrance of the music of life join me with others. Let me not be afraid of the thunder, but see the transforming power of your outstretched hand. Help me to sing my song through the instruments that You have given me, my heart and soul and mind.

Blessed are You, Adonai, who summons me to praise Your name and have made me an instrument of Your will.

Let even the small rivers and rivulets clap their hands. The mountains shout for joy together

"Come," the psalmist entices all of creation, "come join the joyous celebration that is happening now and every day! Just as the huge seas and oceans can participate, so too can the rivers, streams, and rivulets."

The world for the psalmist is a true theater in the round with every created facet — human beings, mountains, rivers, and streams — fully participating in the wonders of life. The awesome mountains, known for being both intimidating and protective, are invited to come together, from the lowest to the most majestic. And we are summoned to join them.

Close your eyes and envision this magnificent picture.

The seas and the dry lands are making a wondrous thunder, the smaller bodies of water are clapping their hands, and the mountainous heights and depths — like a choir of sopranos, altos, tenors, and basses — are shouting for joy.

The Hebrew poets would later write: "This is the day that the LORD has made, be glad and rejoice in it!" There is joy in the smallest and the seemingly least significant of things, says the psalmist. The smallest gesture of caring and the most simple of smiles; the suddenly observed meandering stream — all praise and recognize God. A brief walk or phone call or viewing a budding flower — all this is the joy He would have us see and share.

As we journey through aging, we sometimes question our worth. We may see ourselves as a small rivulet rather than as a roaring sea. Yet it is important to remember that the small tributaries flow out to the larger rivers and seas. Individual drops of water over a period of time can erode a sharp rock — or nourish an arid desert or soul.

FOR FURTHER REFLECTION

1. *"The world is charged with the grandeur of God," wrote the great Catholic poet Gerard Manley Hopkins. "It will flame out, like shining from shook foil" ("God's Grandeur"). Have you ever stood before a day in which God's glory seemed to be blazing on every side? As though the beauty of creation simply could not contain itself? When even the slap of water against the rocks of a stream sounded like hands clapping together? Have you ever felt like joining in the applause? Do you ever feel as though you could burst with gratitude?*

2. *Sometimes the beauty is quieter and more subtle and requires closer attention. And even in those places where human beings may have smudged the beauty of creation, there lives, says the poet Hopkins, "the dearest freshness deep down things." Have you ever felt this? Have you ever seen a little flower growing out of a crack in an ugly wall? Where might you look for "the dearest freshness deep down things" in your life and your surroundings?*

3. *The psalmist wants us — and all of nature — to rejoice and to celebrate life and the Creator and Sustainer of life. As you*

look at your own life, what were some of the mountainous moments, the high points? What is the high point in your life today? When do you feel like a "larger than life" mountain, and when do you feel like an almost imperceptible rivulet? When do you feel significant? When important?

4. *Can you remember a time when life moved slowly and deliberately almost like a small rivulet or creek running through the woods? Was it a sad journey — a happy one — just a pleasant, peaceful time?*

5. *How does time flow for you today? Is it slow, fast, belabored? Do you take the time just to reflect on your day, week, feelings, and thoughts?*

6. *As you look at your life, can you "sit at the river's edge" and enjoy the stream that is flowing by? When does your life flow freely like a river, and when does it move slowly like a rivulet? Do you ever feel that life has passed you by?*

7. *The poet William Wordsworth wrote:*

> *The stars of midnight shall be dear*
> *To her; and she shall lean her ear*
> *In many a secret place*
> *Where rivulets dance their wayward round,*

And beauty born of murmuring sound
Shall pass into her face.

("Three Years She Grew in Sun and Shower")

How do these lines speak to you?

PRAYER

Psalm 98

O Lord, sometimes the thought of being surrounded by the mountains gives me a feeling of safety and security. I feel protected from the elements and dangers from the outside. At other times, I feel confined within barriers I have not chosen. Sometimes I want to hear all of nature shouting for joy; but the joy is muffled or just beyond my reach. I feel overpowered by a discord I can neither deny nor prevent. Sometimes I feel as one of the lowest among your creatures, though I aspire to be among the highest. Help me this day to feel the protection that surrounds me — more than that which confines me. Help me to add my voice, weak as it may be, to the chorus seeking joy. Blessed are You, Adonai, who does hear all my prayers.

Before Adonai, for He comes to judge the earth:
He will judge the world with righteousness,
The people with directness

Now we are told another reason why it is so important that we sing a "new song." God is coming to judge the Earth, and the power of our song and the sound of our music will usher Him in. Every living creature and every creation will lift its voice to create a choir of exultation. None will be left out; even those who have no voice or strength will be included in the judgment and the joy.

Like my one-year-old grandson, Jacob, there are people who make no intelligible sounds with their vocal chords but whose eyes sing a sweet song that would rival any of those attributed to King David. Choirs, symphonies, eyes, and souls will sing a new song of rejoicing, and God in His mercy will judge all the peoples of the world with righteousness and justice. Judgment is what we all want and fear at the same time. We want to be seen in a positive light by our family and friends and God; and we fear that we will be judged harshly and unfairly. As we age, the judgment of others and often of ourselves feels harsh. We can grow from a caring judgment; and we can shrink from an insensitive judgment. The judgment of others does matter, but the judgment of God is always righteous. If the psalmist were an advertising executive, he would take out a large billboard. It would say, "God is coming at a time and in a place near you. Are you ready and open to meet God?"

A phrase in the Hebrew prayer book says that "on that day Adonai will be one and His name will be one." I believe that at the end of time, all people will come to understand that God is the unity behind everything and within everything. While He will be called by many names, just as we are many things to many different people throughout our lives, all will agree that the one God is a God of justice and mercy, and truly a new song, beyond anything we can imagine, will be sung to the Lord.

FOR FURTHER REFLECTION

1. *The psalmist envisions God coming to act in merciful and just ways. In life, sometimes, there are experiences that are*

not just or merciful. Can you describe a time that felt unjust to you and how you overcame it? Do you feel justly treated? Do you treat your caregivers in just and merciful ways? Where is justice lacking in the larger world? Where is it lacking in your world?

2. What feels merciful in your life today? What feels unjust? How can you bring a sense of justice or mercy to another?

3. The coming of God in the final day will bring justice and mercy. It will also mean the fulfillment of His promises, as the psalms, and also prophets like Isaiah, say in many places. Do you think of God as a "keeper of promises"? Do you think of his faithfulness to you? How can a sense of that faithfulness sustain you and guide you in your life today?

———✦———

PRAYER

O God, let my body be an instrument that sings to you in the early morning and in the lateness and lingering hours of the night. Let my voice, however strong or weak, join the chorus that would praise You and all that You have created. Let me recall and know again your mercy and judgment — and even hear you say,

"You are my beloved." Then we shall sing together a song that has no words, because none will be necessary. Blessed are you, Adonai, who at all times calls me Dodi — "My Beloved."

Psalm 98

———

The Psalms in Hebrew

Psalm 121

אשא עיני אל־ההרים מאין יבא עזרי: 1

עזרי מעם יהוה עשה שמים וארץ: 2

אל־יתן למוט רגלך אל־ינום שמרך: 3

הנה לא־ינום ולא יישן שומר ישראל: 4

יהוה שמרך יהוה צלך על־יד ימינך: 5

יומם השמש לא־יככה וירח בלילה: 6

יהוה ישמרך מכל־רע ישמר את־נפשך: 7

יהוה ישמר־צאתך ובואך מעתה ועד־עולם: 8

Psalm 121

1 esa aanay el-hehareem
maa-ayin yavo ezri
2 ezri maa-im adonai
oseh shamayim va-arets
3 al-yitaan lamot raglecha
al-yanum shomerecha
4 hinaa lo-yanum
velo yeeshan shomer yisra-aal
5 adonai shomerecha
adonai tsilecha al-yad yemeenecha
6 yomam hashemesh lo-yakekah
veyaraa-ach balaylah
7 adonai yishmorecha mikol-ra
yishmor et-nafshecha
8 adonai yishmor tsaatecha uvo-echa
maa-atah ve-ad-olam

Psalm 23

1 יהוה רעי לא אחסר:

2 בנאות דשא ירביצני על־מי מנחות ינהלני:

3 נפשי ישובב ינחני במעגלי־צדק למען שמו:

4 גם כי־אלך בגיא צלמות לא־אירא רע

כי־אתה עמדי שבטך ומשענתך המה ינחמני:

5 תערך לפני שלחן נגד צררי

דשנת בשמן ראשי כוסי רויה:

6 אך טוב וחסד ירדפוני כל־ימי חיי

ושבתי בבית־יהוה לארך ימים:

Psalm 23

¹ adonai ro-ee lo echsar

² binot deshe yarbeetsaanee
al maa menuchot yenahalaanee

³ nafshee yeshovaav
yanchaanee vemagelaa tsedeq
lema-an shemo

⁴ gam kee aalaach begaa tsalmavet
lo eera ra kee atah imadi
shivtecha umishantecha
haamah yenachamunee

⁵ ta-aroch lefanay shulchan neged tsoreray
dishanta vashemen roshee kosee revayah

⁶ ach tov vachesed yirdefunee
kol yemaa chayay
veshavti bevaat adonai le-orech yameem

Psalm 98

1 שירו ליהוה שיר חדש כי־נפלאות עשה
הושיעה־לו ימינו וזרוע קדשו:

2 הודיע יהוה ישועתו לעיני הגוים גלה צדקתו:

3 זכר חסדו ואמונתו לבית ישראל
ראו כל־אפסי־ארץ את ישועת אלהינו:

4 הריעו ליהוה כל־הארץ פצחו ורננו וזמרו:

5 זמרו ליהוה בכנור בכנור וקול זמרה:

6 בחצצרות וקול שופר הריעו לפני המלך יהוה:

7 ירעם הים ומלאו תבל וישבי בה:

8 נהרות ימחאו־כף יחד הרים ירננו:

9 לפני־יהוה כי בא לשפט הארץ
ישפט־תבל בצדק ועמים במישרים:

Psalm 98

1 shiru ladonai shir chadash
  kee nifla-ot asah
  hoshee-ah lo yemeeno uzro-a qodsho
2 hodee-a adonai yeshu-ato
  le-aanaa hagoyim gilah tsidqato
3 zakar chasdo ve-emunato levaat yisra-aal
  rau kol afsaa arets aat yeshu-at elohaanu
4 haree-u ladonai kol ha-arets
  pitschu veranenu vezamaaru
5 zameru ladonai bekinor
  bekinor veqol zimrah
6 bachatsotserot veqol shofar
  haree-u lifnaa hamelech adonai
7 yiram hayam umlo-o
  taavaal veyoshevaa vah
8 neharot yimcha-u chaf
  yachad hareem yeranaanu
9 lifnaa adonai
  kee va lishpot ha-arets
  yishpot taavaal betsedeq
  ve-amim bemaashareem

FOR FURTHER READING

Address, Richard F., and Hara E. Person, eds. *That You May Live Long: Caring for Our Aging Parents, Caring for Ourselves.* New York: Union of American Hebrew Congregations Press, 2003.

Bianchi, Eugene C. *Aging as a Spiritual Journey.* New York: Crossroad, 1986.

Brueggemann, Walter. *The Message of the Psalms: A Theological Commentary.* Minneapolis: Augsburg Publishing House, 1984.

Buechner, Frederick. *Listening to Your Life.* San Francisco: HarperSanFrancisco, 1992.

Davidson, Robert. *The Vitality of Worship: A Commentary on the Book of Psalms.* Grand Rapids: Eerdmans, 1998.

Dosick, Rabbi Wayne. *Living Judaism: The Complete Guide to*

Jewish Belief, Tradition, and Practice. San Francisco: HarperSanFrancisco, 1995.

Fox, Matthew. *On Becoming a Musical, Mystical Bear: Spirituality American Style.* New York: Paulist Press, 1976.

Gates of Prayer: The New Union Prayerbook. New York: Central Conference of American Rabbis, 1975.

Goldman, Robert N. *Einstein's God: Albert Einstein's Quest as a Scientist and as a Jew to Replace a Forsaken God.* Northvale, NJ: Jason Aronson, Inc., 1997.

Goodhill, Ruth Marcus, ed. *The Wisdom of Heschel.* New York: Farrar, Straus and Giroux, 1975.

Helminiak, Daniel. *Spiritual Development: An Interdisciplinary Study.* Chicago: Loyola University Press, 1987.

Heschel, Abraham Joshua. *God in Search of Man: A Philosophy of Judaism.* New York: Farrar, Straus and Giroux, 1976.

———. *Man Is Not Alone: A Philosophy of Religion.* New York: Octagon Books, 1972.

———. *Man's Quest for God: Studies in Prayer and Symbolism.* New York: Scribner, 1954.

———. *A Passion for Truth.* Woodstock, VT: Jewish Lights Publishing, 1995.

Kushner, Lawrence. *God Was in This Place and I, I Did Not*

Know: Finding Self, Spirituality, and Ultimate Meaning. Woodstock, VT: Jewish Lights Publishing, 1994.

Lewis, C. S. *Mere Christianity.* New York: Macmillan, 1952.

————. *Reflections on the Psalms.* New York: Harcourt, Brace, 1958.

————. *Surprised by Joy: The Shape of My Early Life.* New York: Harcourt, Brace, 1955.

Merkle, John C. *The Genesis of Faith: The Depth Theology of Abraham Joshua Heschel.* New York: Macmillan, 1985.

Muller, Wayne. *How Then Shall We Live? Four Simple Questions That Reveal the Beauty and Meaning of Our Lives.* New York: Bantam Books, 1997.

Nouwen, Henri J. M. *Lifesigns: Intimacy, Fecundity, and Ecstasy in Christian Perspective.* Garden City, N.Y.: Doubleday, 1986.

————. *The Return of the Prodigal Son: A Story of Homecoming.* New York: Doubleday, 1994.

Nouwen, Henri J. M., and Walter J. Gaffney. *Aging.* New York: Doubleday, 1990.

Ochs, Carol, Kerry M. Olitzky, and Joshua Satzman, eds. *Paths of Faithfulness: Personal Essays on Jewish Spirituality.* Hoboken, NJ: KTAV Publishing House, 1997.

Palmer, Parker J. *Let Your Life Speak: Listening for the Voice of Vocation.* San Francisco: Jossey-Bass, 2000.

Polish, Daniel F. *Bringing the Psalms to Life: How to Understand and Use the Book of Psalms.* Woodstock, VT: Jewish Lights Publishing, 2000.

Rosten, Leo. *Treasury of Jewish Quotations.* New York: McGraw Hill, 1972.